CLAYTON & SHARIE KING

GROUNDED

for real life

WISDOM FROM PROVERBS AND JAMES

LifeWay | Students

STUDENT MINISTRY PUBLISHING

BEN TRUEBLOOD
Director,
Student Ministry

JOHN PAUL BASHAM
Manager,
Student Ministry Publishing

KAREN DANIEL
Editorial Team Leader

ANDY MCLEAN
Content Editor

STEPHANIE LIVENGOOD
Production Editor

SARAH NIKOLAI
Graphic Designer

Requests for permission should be addressed in writing to LifeWay Press®, One LifeWay Plaza, Nashville, TN 37234.

ISBN: 978-1-4300-6457-2
Item Number: 005791911

Dewey Decimal Classification Number: 242.2
Subject Heading: DEVOTIONAL LITERATURE/ BIBLE STUDY AND TEACHING / GOD

Printed in the United States of America.

Student Ministry Publishing
LifeWay Resources
One LifeWay Plaza
Nashville, TN 37234

We believe that the Bible has God for its author; salvation for its end; and truth, without any mixture of error, for its matter and that all Scripture is totally true and trustworthy. To review LifeWay's doctrinal guideline, please visit www.lifeway.com/doctrinalguideline.

TABLE OF CONTENTS

ABOUT THE AUTHORS

CLAYTON KING serves as a Teaching Pastor at NewSpring Church in Anderson, South Carolina. In addition to his leadership role there, he spends his time traveling, preaching, and speaking in churches, conferences, and leadership events, as well as running Crossroads/Clayton King Ministries, which is the non-profit organization he founded in 1995. His ministry offers summer camps, student conferences, and leadership and coaching networks. He is married to Sharie, and they enjoy working, writing, and speaking together. He loves good books, black coffee, four-wheelers and anything that gets him outside and in the woods.

SHARIE KING married Clayton in 1999. She's the co-founder of Crossroads Summer Camps and Clayton King Ministries. Sharie felt a call into ministry at age 12 and has traveled to over 20 countries serving the nations and sharing the gospel. She blogs regularly at sharieking.com and hosts a podcast called *Overcoming Monday*. She loves to paint, snow ski, and spend time with her family. She and Clayton are parents to two teenage sons, Jacob and Joseph.

INTRODUCTION

In 1 Kings 3, God asked King Solomon what He could give Solomon as he stepped into this newly appointed position of king over Israel. Wow, what an offer! God, the Creator and Sustainer of the universe, asked Solomon how He could help with his new job as leader of God's people. Solomon could have asked for all sorts of things, but he chose to request wisdom. He could have asked God for an army that would never be defeated or for his own longevity as king, but again—he didn't. Solomon knew enough about being king to realize he desperately needed God's help if he wanted to be a faithful king like his father, David. Instead of offering up a self-serving prayer that would only benefit him, Solomon asked for wisdom to lead God's people well. Sure, wisdom would help him, but he also saw it as a way to help the people he was leading.

Solomon's situation isn't too different from our own. No, we may not be leaders to masses of people like Solomon, but we desperately need God's help to know how to live on a daily basis. Because of that, our prayer should be that God would grant us His wisdom.

HOW TO USE

This book contains eight weekly group studies. Each group study is designed to be one hour, with about 10-15 minutes of video teaching and 45 minutes of group interaction/discussion.

Each session consists of an overview, a watch page, a group discussion guide, and four days of personal study. There is also a leader guide at the back of this study with helpful tips to use during group time. As you finish each group session, encourage students to complete the personal studies and devotions on their own.

START

This page includes a brief summary of the lesson to introduce the video segment.

WATCH

This page includes key points from the video teaching, along with space for taking notes as participants watch the video.

DISCUSS

These two pages include questions and statements that guide the group into further study of the topic through additional Bible passages and questions.

PERSONAL STUDY

Each session contains four days of personal study that follows every session. Be sure to work through these in the days leading to the next session. Allow for some time at the beginning of each session to discuss what was learned during these personal study days.

DEVOTIONS

In addition to Personal Study days, 30 days of devotions are included in the back of the book so students can continue their study of Proverbs and James on their own after completing the group sessions.

START

What is wisdom? Some people point to knowledge and information. Others may think of wisdom as life experience. Still, a few might recall one-liners similar to what you might find in fortune cookies. In this session, we see that God has given us His Word to teach us how to walk in wisdom. As we dig into the Book of Proverbs, we learn that wisdom is rooted in the fear of the Lord, how it leads us to trust in God, and how it offers us practical guidance for everyday life. Ultimately, wisdom isn't *something* but *someone*—Jesus. In Jesus we have the very wisdom and Word of God, which means if we want to become wise, we need to first have a relationship with Him.

WATCH

Fill in the blanks to follow along as you watch the Session 1 video.

1. If wisdom is a priceless buried treasure, then the fear of the Lord is the map and the road that takes you there.

2. There is a reverence for the power of God that should always follow a revelation of the character of God.

3. The best thing you can do for yourself is to fear the Lord.

4. Wisdom is about fearing the right things. When you fear God, you don't have to be afraid of anything else.

Discuss

1. Who in your life displays biblical wisdom consistently in their actions? What are some characteristics you admire about those people? How do they display a healthy fear and reverence of God?

2. How has this session challenged you when it comes to thinking about wisdom and how wisdom is attained in someone's life?

Answers: 1) map, road; 2) power, character; 3) fear 4) fearing, afraid of

GROUP DISCUSSION

Read Proverbs 1:1-7.

> *The proverbs of Solomon son of David, king of Israel: For learning wisdom and discipline; for understanding insightful sayings; for receiving prudent instruction in righteousness, justice, and integrity; for teaching shrewdness to the inexperienced, knowledge and discretion to a young man—let a wise person listen and increase learning, and let a discerning person obtain guidance—for understanding a proverb or a parable, the words of the wise, and their riddles. The fear of the Lord is the beginning of knowledge; fools despise wisdom and discipline.*
> —Proverbs 1:1-7

What's the difference between worldly "wisdom" and biblical wisdom?

How do these verses describe wisdom?

Do you think being wise is more than knowing lots of information? Why or why not?

Notice how these verses relate being wise to receiving information. Wisdom involves understanding insightful sayings, instruction, learning, and knowledge. But wisdom is more than information, though it is certainly not less. Although wisdom involves information, it would be wrong to assume someone is wise just because he or she has a lot of information. Solomon said wisdom is rooted in the fear of the Lord (v. 7), which means we need to start with God if we want to possess true wisdom and knowledge.

Where do you think most people turn for instruction and advice today?

How might those voices of influence and authority be different for Christians?

Wisdom starts with a relationship with God. He is the source of all wisdom, insight, and knowledge. Think about that: God knows all things! He never has a new thought. He is never surprised by new information. He knows all information perfectly. When we're looking for advice or instruction, He isn't just one option among many—He is our only option.

The Book of Proverbs describes a foolish person as one who doesn't fear the Lord. Since they don't fear the Lord—the source of wisdom—they naturally despise wisdom.

Read Proverbs 3:1-8.

> *My son, don't forget my teaching, but let your heart keep my commands; for they will bring you many days, a full life, and well-being. Never let loyalty and faithfulness leave you. Tie them around your neck; write them on the tablet of your heart. Then you will find favor and high regard with God and people. Trust in the LORD with all your heart, and do not rely on your own understanding; in all your ways know him, and he will make your paths straight. Don't be wise in your own eyes; fear the LORD and turn away from evil. This will be healing for your body and strengthening for your bones.* —Proverbs 3:1-8

According to these verses, what does wisdom lead to?

Solomon said wisdom is rooted in the fear of the Lord, and our fear of the Lord must translate into a rock solid faith in God. In other words, wisdom leads to a life that demonstrates faith in God.

What are some characteristics of a life lived by faith?

Look at the connection Solomon made here. If wisdom leads to a life of faith in God, then that faith will demonstrate dependence upon God in all things. This kind of faith leads us to look to God and trust in Him, rather than looking inward and being self-reliant. It will lead us to rely on the clarity, direction, and understanding only God can give instead of trusting our own smarts or giftedness.

In what areas of life are you tempted to rely on yourself instead of God? Why do you think we are tempted to be self-reliant and independent from God?

Where do you need God's wisdom in your own life (relationships or otherwise)?

Wisdom is about truth in action. God not only wants us to *know* the truth, but He wants us to *live* the truth. This is why the book of Proverbs is an extremely practical book. Sure, it teaches us to know certain things, but it also teaches us to do certain things. God, through the wisdom he gave to Solomon, intended for his hearers to live out the truths contained in these proverbs.

Read Proverbs 22:1-10.

A good name is to be chosen over great wealth; favor is better than silver and gold. Rich and poor have this in common: the LORD makes them all. A sensible person sees danger and takes cover, but the inexperienced keep going and are punished. Humility, the fear of the LORD, results in wealth, honor, and life. There are thorns and snares on the way of the crooked; the one who guards himself stays far from them. Start a youth out on his way; even when he grows old he will not depart from it. The rich rule over the poor, and the borrower is a slave to the lender. The one who sows injustice will reap disaster, and the rod of his fury will be destroyed. A generous person will be blessed, for he shares his food with the poor. Drive out a mocker, and conflict goes too; then quarreling and dishonor will cease. —Proverbs 22:1-10

In space below, summarize in your own words what Solomon challenged us to do in each verse:

v. 1:

v. 2:

v. 3:

v. 4:

v. 5:

v. 6:

v. 7:

v. 8:

v. 9:

v. 10:

Consider the areas mentioned in just these few verses and how important wisdom is to each one. The danger here is that we would only read and hear these, maybe study them more in-depth, but never actually apply them to our daily lives. Wisdom is about transformation, not just information. Wisdom is mean to do more than take up space in our minds; it's meant to be lived out as a result of a transformed heart that is completely and totally dependent upon God. It begins on a personal level with an internal fear and love for God, which expresses itself externally in the way it shapes a person's actions each day.

How has this session challenged you when it comes to pursuing biblical wisdom in your own life?

How can you seek to grow in wisdom this week?

PERSONAL STUDY

DAY 1

Now if any of you lacks wisdom, he should ask God—who gives to all generously and ungrudgingly—and it will be given to him. –James 1:5

How do you usually get something you really want? You ask, and then you go for it.

When I was 15 years old, I wanted a car, but I really wanted a Camaro. Since I knew my parents wouldn't buy it for me, I decided to buy it myself. That would mean making money, which would mean hard work. I would have to take on an extra job. I would have to save up everything I made. I couldn't spend all my cash going out with my friends. Buying my own car would require a lot from me.

In other words, when I decided I wanted a Camaro, I had to choose to pursue it. I went after it! I made phone calls and got extra jobs. I cut grass, hauled trash, and even spread black tar on driveways in 100 degree heat. My pursuit paid off when I paid for my 1979 black Camaro with cash! To get what I wanted, I had to decide to pursue it. Wisdom works the same way—if you want to be grounded in it, you have to go after it. The first step is to ask God to help you. He will give you the wisdom you need, because He's the only source of real wisdom in the entire universe.

What are you pursuing right now?

What do you spend most of your free time doing?

When have you made up your mind to pursue something and it worked out?

Have you ever failed when you pursued something? How did that feel? How did you respond?

What would your spiritual life look like if you got serious about pursuing wisdom?

How much time do you spend (on average) reading Scripture every day?

How would your life change if you doubled or tripled the amount of time you spend reading and studying the Bible?

DAY 2

What would you be willing to give up in order to get something you really want?

Proverbs says even if it costs us everything, we must gain wisdom. That's a rather strong statement to make. It assumes wisdom is more valuable than pretty much anything we have. So, what would you be willing to give up to get wisdom?

When Clayton's dad died, he left us a small sum of money with the instruction to buy some four wheelers for our family. My kids were really into ATVs (all-terrain vehicles) at the time, and we lived on a big farm in North Carolina where we had plenty of room to ride them. We had hours of fun and got muddy from head to toe. Then we moved to South Carolina. We no longer had a big farm with lots of trails. My boys were more into sports and church. So we decided we would sell the ATVs and use the money for something even more fun; a family trip to Hawaii.

We gave up something we had for something we wanted. The trip was amazing. We swam with sharks. We went snorkeling. We hiked dormant volcanoes. And we gained memories that we will never, ever forget (and some really cool pictures).

Wisdom is more valuable than anything you currently have in your life; without wisdom, you can't make the good choices that allow you to enjoy the rest of the life God has given you. So it makes sense to prioritize wisdom over everything else.

Think about the thing you want most right now (a trip to the beach over spring break, a Ferrari, the newest smart phone, etc.). How much do you think that would cost?

What do you think is the average cost of tuition at your dream college? Now take a minute to look it up, and write down that answer.

What are some things in life that you love or enjoy that are free (clean air, exercise, being outside, etc.)?

What do you think it costs to gain wisdom?

Is there a dollar amount you have to pay to become wise? Why or why not?

DAY 3

Proverbs 1:7 says fools despise correction and instruction. That's a bold statement. Can you imagine calling someone a fool to their face? Or can you imagine being called a fool by someone, especially someone you respect or look up to? In our politically correct culture, it's rare to hear such a strong word used to describe someone. So why does the Bible use it?

The Book of Proverbs uses the word fool more than once, actually. Wisdom and foolishness are compared over and over again, as are wise people and fools. God uses such a strong word in Proverbs for effect. Wisdom is so important to God that He chooses to use a word that is sure to get your attention. He's not being mean; He's being loving and honest. But don't get sidetracked by the force of the word *fool*. Instead, decide not to walk the path of foolishness, not to ignore the wisdom of God and His Word.

Proverbs 17:28 says, "Even a fool is considered wise when he keeps silent–discerning, when he seals his lips." The meaning here is simple–when you spend all your time talking, you can't hear anything anyone is saying to you. That's what fools do. So, the first step to ending your foolish ways is to be stop talking and be quiet so you can actually hear what God is trying to teach you. Even fools can become wise they will close their mouths and open their ears.

How would you react if someone called you a fool?

Are you acting in foolish ways right now that you will later regret?

Do you show signs of wisdom or foolishness by the way you react to older people when they give you advice about your decisions?

What barriers in your life right now are holding you back from pursuing God's wisdom?

DAY 4

One who listens to life-giving rebukes will be at home among the wise. Anyone who ignores discipline despises himself, but whoever listens to correction acquires good sense. –Proverbs 15:31-32

Growing up, I played all three major sports (football, basketball, and baseball). At a young age, I became accustomed to what it was like to be under the authority of an older man. I got used to having a coach. It was his job to instruct us, to correct us, and to train our team to execute the rules of whatever sport we were playing. I loved some of my coaches and others weren't exactly my favorite. But they all had one thing in common, from little league all the way through my final high school football season: They knew more than I did.

Why would I possibly resist the wisdom and knowledge of a coach who sees what I don't see and understands what I don't understand? That would be the definition of foolish. That is exactly what Proverbs warns against repeatedly. God has complete knowledge of all things. He's been around longer than anyone, so His experience is unparalleled. Therefore, He is the Person you need to go to first when you're confused or struggling in any area of your life. Whether it's temptation or conflict with your parents, or feelings of insecurity, or an addiction—there is no One better equipped to coach you through it than God Himself.

Have you ever acted in a foolish way and regretted it later? What happened?

What is your first internal reaction when someone corrects you? Do you get upset?

Why do you think it's so easy to reject the instruction and correction of those who are older and wiser than you?

WISE COUNSEL

START

Knowing how to live out a godly life in Christ doesn't come naturally. Sure, believers have the Holy Spirit to guide us as we read and search the Scriptures for ourselves. But God designed His children to grow and mature their faith in the context of community. As one generation speaks truth and wisdom into the lives of another generation, God's divine design of wise counsel takes place. In this session, we will see the benefits of seeking out older, mature, godly examples to look to and imitate in the faith, resulting in greater devotion as a disciple of Christ.

WATCH

Fill in the blanks to follow along as you watch the Session 2 video.

1. There is a difference between knowledge and wisdom. Knowledge is about knowing *facts*, but wisdom is about knowing *what's best*.

2. Wise counsel means a collective voice of people that *know* God and His Word and can impart such *understanding* to you.

3. The great strength of seeking out the counsel of others is that it *protects* you from missing the *blind spots* in your own life.

4. Many of us have *knowledge* but we lack *wisdom* simply because we know what we should do but we don't actually do it.

5. The goal of gaining wisdom is not *intellect*; it's *intimacy*.

Discuss

1. Describe a time when God used someone to speak much needed wisdom into your life. Then share about a time when you shared wisdom with someone by giving them helpful advice.

2. How has this session challenged you when it comes to thinking about seeking out wisdom from others in your own life?

Answers: 1) facts, what's best; 2) know, understanding; 3) protects, blind spots; 4) knowledge, wisdom; 5) intellect, intimacy

GROUP DISCUSSION

Learning from others is a key part to growing in wisdom and being disciples of Christ. As disciples, we constantly learn from others who are older and more mature in the faith, but we also look behind us for opportunities to make disciples of the next generation.

Why are we tempted to believe we don't need the counsel of wise, godly people speaking into our lives?

What are some ways you have been discipled? What are some ways you have contributed to the discipleship of others?

Read Deuteronomy 6:4-7.

"Listen, Israel: The LORD our God, the LORD is one. Love the LORD your God with all your heart, with all your soul, and with all your strength. These words that I am giving you today are to be in your heart. Repeat them to your children. Talk about them when you sit in your house and when you walk along the road, when you lie down and when you get up." –Deuteronomy 6:4-7

What stands out to you in these verses?

Parents were encouraged to teach the principles they received from God through Moses in everyday circumstances. They were called to teach Gods ways all the time. Why? Because our hearts are stubborn, and we have to learn and relearn how to walk with God and live out His Word.

Because of this stubbornness and hardness of heart, we need godly people in our lives who genuinely love and care about us and will speak the truth to us. We need their counsel, just like the children of Moses' day needed their parents to provide the counsel they needed to faithfully follow after God.

When does Moses say instruction should take place? Why is this significant?

Take a look at when Moses told these parents and leaders to pass on the wise counsel to the next generation. Was it in the context of a formal Sunday School environment or in the formal structure of a in-home small group? Nope. While there is nothing wrong with these learning environments, Moses wanted to emphasize that godly wisdom and counsel are to take place at all times, even in the most common everyday experiences—hanging out at home, on the road, or getting ready for bed. In other words, gaining wisdom from wise counsel shouldn't just happen during the service on Sunday morning; it should happen in the most ordinary circumstances of everyday life as we surround ourselves with wise counselors.

What might talking about God's Word with wise counselors look like in your own life and schedule today?

Who speaks wise and godly counsel into your life? If you don't have anyone who does this, who are some older godly people (men for guys and women for girls) you can turn to?

So, we've established that having godly counsel in your life is super important. We've also talked about how this counsel shouldn't just be received through sermons at church, but in the context of a older godly person speaking into your life on a regular basis.

While having someone speak truth into your life is vitally important, wise counsel is more than transferring biblical information from one person to another. It includes imitating others who are imitating Christ. If imitating others is a goal of wise counsel, then having a personal relationship with that wise counselor is essential.

Read 1 Corinthians 4:14-21; 11:1.

I'm not writing this to shame you, but to warn you as my dear children. For you may have countless instructors in Christ, but you don't have many fathers. For I became your father in Christ Jesus through the gospel. Therefore I urge you to imitate me. This is why I have sent Timothy to you. He is my dearly loved and faithful child in the Lord. He will remind you about my ways in Christ Jesus, just as I teach everywhere in every church. –1 Corinthians 4:14-21

Imitate me, as I also imitate Christ. –1 Corinthians 11:1

Do you think it would be strange to ask someone to imitate you? Why or why not?

Ultimately, when you think about it, Paul wasn't asking people to live like him, but rather to live like Jesus. In other words, he was inviting people to come alongside of him to live like the One who called them out of darkness into His marvelous light (1 Pet. 2:9).

When it comes down to it, wise counsel is about being taught something and being shown something. Being a wise counselor means you model what you preach so those who are listening and watching will know what it looks like to live out our faith.

Think about it this way: Consider the difference between telling someone how to change a tire on their car versus showing them how to do it. As you explain the process to them, you would have to describe the tools in detail, know what each part is called, and hope your knowledge of their vehicle allows you to tell them where the spare tire is located (under the car, in the trunk, under the floorboard, or mounted on the back, etc.). In this scenario, merely describing or instructing can be difficult, which is why showing is also vitally important.

Now, read Hebrews 13:7.

*Remember your leaders who have spoken God's word to you. As you carefully observe the outcome of their lives, imitate their faith.
–Hebrews 13:7*

The Bible encourages us to have biblical heroes. Sure, it gives us criteria when choosing who to follow. We should always examine the outcome of their faith by asking questions like, "Are they living what they are preaching?" But once that criteria is meet, we need to make sure we have people like that in our own lives, and that we are becoming like this in someone else's life.

How will others see Christ in your life this week?

PERSONAL STUDY

DAY 1

*A mocker doesn't love one who corrects him; he will not consult
the wise.* —Proverbs 15:12

Does this describe anyone you know? Have you ever seen someone who absolutely cannot stand to be corrected? When a teacher or a coach tries to instruct them about something they did wrong, they begin to make excuses. They blame other people. They deny that they did anything wrong at all. They get visibly upset. They may even lose their temper, yell, or change the subject. The person who reacts to correction with resentment will most definitely never go seeking out wisdom from another person. They resent being told what to do, that resentment is rooted in pride, and pride *always* precedes destruction.

The opposite of this is described in verses 31-32.

One who listens to life-giving rebukes will be at home among the wise. Anyone who ignores discipline despises himself, but whoever listens to correction acquires good sense. —Proverbs 15:31-32

Do you want to be at home among the wise, surrounded by wise friends, and have an ever-increasing capacity for intelligence and good decision-making? If so, just make sure you listen to wiser people when they attempt to correct and guide you. But this actually demands a first step. Before you can listen to wise people as they instruct you, you have to first invite wise people into your life to observe how you live, how you think, how you talk, who you hang out with, and the way you treat others. This means you have to have real relationships with people who are wiser than you. Where can you find people like this? They are part of your church, and hopefully part of your family.

Consult the wise and you will win.

*Plans fail when there is no counsel, but with many advisers
they succeed.* —Proverbs 15:22

Do you actively seek out older, wiser people before you make big decisions?

Do you currently have a mentor—someone who is older and wiser than you—who you can trust?

List the names of two people in your church or family you will invite to be part of your "wise counsel."

DAY 2

A wise son brings joy to his father, but a foolish man despises his mother. —Proverbs 15:20

When you think about seeking out the wisdom of older Christians who can help you plan out a course for your life, one of your goals may be making your parents proud of you. Who doesn't want that? All children grow up wanting their parents to notice them. Every little kid says, "Mama, daddy, watch this!" That phrase may be followed by jumping off the couch onto a bean bag, doing a flip on the trampoline, or tying your shoe for the first time. Kids love to show off for their parents, and parents feel a sense of joy when they see their children developing and growing.

There is literally nothing in this world that brings us more joy than watching our children make good decisions. When we watch them place their tithe in the baskets at church on Sunday, it gives us a deep sense of happiness knowing they're actually doing what we have trained them to do. But our boys chose to listen to us when they were young and that has made all the difference.

However, the most foolish thing you can do is ignore your parents by thinking they're stupid and you know better than they do. Have you ever seen this with some of your friends? They talk about their parents as if they're idiots. Maybe they speak to them disrespectfully, especially when their friends are around. Proverbs says those who despise their parents are fools.

What are some practical ways you can invite your mom and dad to speak into your life?

How much time do you spend actually talking to your parents, without any distractions like TV or your phone?

Do you think your mom or dad would be willing to spend an hour a week eating breakfast or lunch—just the two of you—mentoring you and teaching you life lessons they've learned?

Would you be willing to ask them to do it?

DAY 3

A rebuke impresses a discerning person more than a hundred lashes a fool. —Proverbs 17:10, NIV

What in the world does it mean to be impressed by a rebuke? Well let me ask you this; have you ever been rebuked? I mean, have you ever had someone love you enough to tell you that you were wrong? The Bible says that if you are wise, you will be impressed by someone that isn't worried about hurting your feelings but will tell you the truth about your actions in spite of how you may respond.

This is what wise counsel looks like. A true friend isn't going to let you make a mistake, or date the wrong person, or get in trouble at school, without warning you of what is to come. You may think that your best friends would never hurt your feelings, but in reality the people who truly love you the most are willing to risk offending you to save you from the consequences of doing something foolish or harmful.

I remember when this happened to me in the 11th grade. I was taking Geometry, and there were two guys from my football team in that class. The three of us together was like an explosion waiting to happen. We would play off each other, get really loud and crazy, and end up taking over the class. Our teacher was a sweet lady who loved us, but we would easily overwhelm her with out personalities and our volume.

One day at lunch a really quiet girl from my class sat down beside me in the lunchroom. She was so timid, yet so bold in that moment. She said that we were intimidating our teacher. She knew we didn't mean to, but we were taking over the class every day when we cut up and acted crazy. It was so weird having this tiny, shy girl basically tell me I was wrong. Then she really lowered the hammer on me when she said, "And Clayton, you're a Christian. People know you are because you talk about Jesus all the time. I'm just concerned about your testimony, and I don't want people getting the wrong impression."

Talk about an impression! That was almost 30 years ago and her willingness to lovingly come to me with a rebuke left such an impression on me that I'm still talking about it.

What about other people impresses you?

Have you ever been impressed with someone who is bold enough to confront another person? If so, who was it and what did that person do?

Who do you have in your life that is willing to show you some areas in your life that you may not see?

DAY 4

Who among you is wise and understanding? By his good conduct he should show that his works are done in the gentleness that comes from

wisdom. But if you have bitter envy and selfish ambition in your heart,
don't boast and deny the truth. —James 3:13-14

According to James, the way we prove that we are actually growing in wisdom is by the way we live. In other words, we begin to change our ways and put into practice the things we learn. We do this with humility, not bragging on ourselves or drawing attention to ourselves, but simply acting in ways that glorify God and draw attention to Him and His work in our hearts through the Holy Spirit. The opposite of this posture is the root of pride that leads to bitter envy towards others.

James said when we allow selfish ambition to overtake our hearts, we deny the truth. This means, when we forget our proper place of humility and let jealousy and envy fill our hearts instead, we begin to treat others with contempt and disrespect. When we do this, we aren't representing the truth of the gospel and how Jesus changes our hearts, moving us from being selfish to being servants. We deny the truth of what it means to be Christians when we try to elevate ourselves above others. The Christian life is about taking a lower position to bless those around us.

One practical way we maintain humility and fight selfish ambition is to remain open to the wisdom of other Christians who can help us see things we might miss. When you isolate yourself from the community of faith, you don't have a reference point to remind you that you're not the most important person in the universe. Your fallen, sinful nature will naturally want you to elevate yourself above others, but the Spirit of God inside of you fights against that desire by leading you to become less. Your brothers and sisters in Christ are often times the means by which the Holy Spirit keeps you in that proper frame of mind.

Have you ever been jealous of another person? Explain.

What do you usually get jealous about (friends, money, abilities, or grades, etc.)?

When did you last celebrate a blessing God gave to one of your friends?

HEART

SESSION THREE

START

The Bible talks a lot about the human heart. Not the muscle responsible for circulating blood throughout the body, although that's important. Instead, the Bible's understanding of the heart refers to the center of a person, the essence of who they are. It describes the heart as being the command center for why people do the things they do. It is the agent behind every spoken word and the ultimate cause behind every careless deed. We might be able to hide the condition of our hearts from others by trying to look good on the outside or doing the right things, but our hearts eventually reveal what they truly are. This is why wisdom regarding the heart points us to the gospel and the fact that only God can change our hearts.

WATCH

Fill in the blanks to follow along as you watch the Session 3 video.

1. All real love, emotion, desire, and compassion emanates from the *Heart*.

2. When it's on its own, and not surrendered to God, your heart can do some major *Damage*, both to you and the people around you.

3. God is on a mission to *win* your heart back, to *clense* your heart with His love, and to *fill* your heart with His Spirit.

4. *faith* is how Jesus gets into your heart, and faith is how your heart gets *grounded*. When your heart is grounded, you are grounded.

Discuss

1. How would you explain the connection between a person's heart and behavior?

2. How has this session's video challenged you when it comes to the importance of guarding your own heart?

GROUP DISCUSSION

Proverbs and James emphasize the heart when it comes to the Christian life. But let's take a look outside of those two books to see what the rest of the Bible says about the role of the heart in Christians' lives.

There's no better place about understanding the role of the heart than in the teachings of Jesus Himself. Consider the following passage:

Read Matthew 15:8.

> *"This people honors me with their lips, but their heart is far from me."*
> —Matthew 15:8

What can we learn about the importance of the heart from this short verse?

When it comes to understanding Jesus' meaning here, think about who He was talking to. Jesus was addressing the Pharisees in this passage, a group of extremely religious people in Jesus' day. These people were known for their being outwardly religious, showing off their elaborate prayers in public and their ability to follow all of the nuances of Old Testament laws with extreme devotion and intensity.

This passage reveals that there is a huge difference between being religious and having a heart that is devoted to God. Sure, like countless cultural Christians today these Pharisees talked liked people who knew God. Maybe they even acted like people who knew God. Sadly, they didn't actually know Him. They had spiritual checklists and knew their doctrines, but those weren't enough. Jesus said there was no connection between their religious hearts and God's heart.

Why is it important that our words about God match what we feel about God in our hearts?

When have you been guilty of being simply religious and going through the motions with little to no heart involved? What did you do?

After opening up a discussion about the importance of the heart in His conversation with the Pharisees, Jesus elaborated on the role of the heart.

Read Matthew 15:10-20.

> *Summoning the crowd, he told them, "Listen and understand: It's not what goes into the mouth that defiles a person, but what comes out of the mouth—this defiles a person." Then the disciples came up and told him, "Do you know that the Pharisees took offense when they heard what you said?" He replied, "Every plant that my heavenly Father didn't plant will be uprooted. Leave them alone! They are blind guides. And if the blind guide the blind, both will fall into a pit." Then Peter said, "Explain this parable to us."*
>
> *"Do you still lack understanding?" he asked. "Don't you realize that whatever goes into the mouth passes into the stomach and is eliminated? But what comes out of the mouth comes from the heart, and this defiles a person. For from the heart come evil thoughts, murders, adulteries, sexual immoralities, thefts, false testimonies, slander. These are the things that defile a person; but eating with unwashed hands does not defile a person." –Matthew 15:10-20*

How would you summarize Jesus' teaching on the heart here?

Jesus' teaching about the heart can be summarized with this simple slogan: It's all about the heart!

Think of it this way. Imagine you're walking next to a beautiful, pristine creek one day and notice trash and pollution floating downstream. What would you do? Most people would want to clear the junk from the stream. They grab a trash bag and use a net to "catch" the empty plastic bottles or put on some gloves and pick up the trash with their bare hands. All is well and good, but that doesn't correct the problem. Providing a permanent solution would require finding the source—traveling upstream to where it all started.

The same is for us. We can try to correct our bad behavior (trash) but unless we deal with the heart behind those behaviors (source), we'll never have a permanent solution.

Shortly before this incident, Jesus made the connection between words and the heart, saying, "the mouth speaks from the overflow of the heart" (Matt. 12:34). Here, Jesus only built on that connection by showing how all of the actions we take find their root cause within the recesses of our hearts.

Have you ever thought about the connection between your speech and your heart?

If our speech provides us with a mirror of the condition of our hearts, then how does the way you talk to others and about others reveal about the current state of your heart?

In light of the role of the heart when it comes to our speech and behavior, do you consider this good news or bad news? Explain.

The Bible's emphasis on the heart is both good news and bad news. The bad news is religious and ritualistic behavior won't protect us from sin and evil, just like the Pharisees' observing laws didn't protect them from sin and evil.

The good news is we know where the problem actually lies—deep within us. It's not so much that we are fighting against some external sin and evil; instead, we are recognizing an natural bent towards sin and evil within our own hearts. It's good to know where the issue is, even if it hurts to find out the problem lies within.

The emphasis on the heart is also good news because it tells us that we can't do anything on our own to change our hearts. Only Jesus can change our hearts. This is exactly what God promised in the New Covenant when He said He would take away our hearts of stone and give us hearts of flesh (Ezek. 11:19). Once we realize Jesus is our only cure to the heart disease we all have, we're even more grateful for His sacrifice and our salvation.

How would you explain to someone the importance of focusing primarily on the internal issue of the heart versus external problems of behavior?

What happens if we neglect the heart when dealing with behavioral problems in our lives?

PERSONAL STUDY

DAY 1

A joyful heart is good medicine, but a broken spirit dries up the bones.
–Proverbs 17:22

What is a broken spirit and how does it dry up your bones? A broken spirit is a deep feeling of sadness or disappointment, a sense that things are bad and they're not getting better. Some would call it depression. I understand that feeling. Shortly after our first son was born, I couldn't figure out what was wrong with me. My mind and my body ached, all the way down to the bones. It felt like my bones and my spirit were drying up inside of me, and I began to understand what this verse meant. Clayton encouraged me to see a Christian counselor, and I did. Then Clayton and I went together and it helped us make sense of what I was going through.

I was experiencing depression. Much of it was due to the chemical and hormonal changes in my body after having a baby. Finding out the "why" behind how I was feeling was most helpful. Then, the counselor told us to have fun. Because I was so sad, having fun seemed impossible at the time. I couldn't remember how it felt to laugh or truly have a good time, but we decided we would try.

We went out on a date. We ate dinner and talked. We saw a movie. We took a walk. Over time, I could feel my heart begin to lose the heavy weight holding it down, and I started to enjoy life again. I found joy again in being a mom and loving my little boy. As the postpartum depression went away, the joy in my heart felt like good medicine, but not the kind a doctor prescribes to you. It was the kind that only God can give. My broken spirit was slowly healed by the good medicine of a joyful heart.

Do you ever feel depressed? If so, describe what kinds of thoughts and feelings you experience.

What are some things that fill your heart with joy?

List some things or people you think drag you down and make your heart feel heavy and sad.

List some things and some people that lift your spirits and make you feel positive, encouraged, and happy.

DAY 2

The mind of the discerning acquires knowledge, and the ear of the wise seeks it. —Proverbs 18:15

For years our family has dreamed of going on an African safari. Clayton lived in Kenya for a while in college and told us about a day-long safari he took, which just made us want to go that much more.

Our dream came true when our boys were 12 and 15. We all went to Uganda together, and Clayton was able to preach in Nelson Mandela Stadium to over 100,000 people. As a treat, we spent five days in South Africa on a safari. Our guide picked us up every morning and evening, and drove us around the mountains and valleys of Pilansberg National Park where we saw every kind of African animal imaginable. It was breathtaking!

I remember most vividly how our guide had trained her eyes and ears to see and hear things we didn't recognize. She could hear lions roar from miles away. She could see giraffes miles in the distance. Her ears and eyes were unbelievably attuned to her surroundings.

How did she become so perceptive? How did she train her vision and hearing to become so sharp? Simply put, she practiced, and the practice made perfect. Every day, she would load families into her jeep and drive the roads of Pilansberg, watching the game trails and listening for the sounds rhinos made as they walked through the bush or elephants as they crashed through acacia trees. The more she used her eyes and ears, the sharper they became. She naturally noticed the sounds and sights of the African plains as she acquired the ability to discern between the different movements and sounds of the bush.

This is how we acquire knowledge. Our ears seek it out. Our eyes learn to look for it. We glean wisdom from every possible source, beginning with the Bible. We slow down long enough to perceive what God is telling us. We listen more than we talk, we ask questions, we read, we journal, and we learn from older mentors.

Name five of the best sources of wisdom.

Do you think time on your phone makes you wiser? Why or why not?

How much time each day do you spend on social media or the internet?

DAY 3

All a person's ways seem right to him, but the LORD weighs hearts.
—Proverbs 21:2

What does it mean when this verse says that the Lord "weighs" our hearts? How much does an actual heart weigh? Is that what this means?

Actually, that's not what this means at all. This literally means God knows the motives of our hearts. He understands why we do the things we do and if we do them for the right reasons or the wrong reasons. It's a good thing to do the right thing.

Do you know what is even better than doing the right thing? Doing the right thing for the right reason.

We can't always tell the true motivation behind our good actions, and we often find ourselves doing something good so we will look good or others will see us and be impressed with us. We all want to put our best foot forward. We want others to think highly of us. Yet we often make mistakes because we make decisions based on how we can get something we want rather what is best for someone else. That is the definition of selfishness. I admit that I don't always notice how selfishness motivates me. Only God can weigh the motives of my heart.

When we gossip about others behind their back, we show what's really in our hearts. We want to make another person look bad so we feel better about ourselves. When we are secretly jealous or envious of a brother or sister in Christ, we reveal that our hearts are insecure and our identity is based on something other than being God's child.

It's natural to hide selfish motives deep in our hearts. We all make mistakes and realize that we do things for the wrong reasons. Open your heart to the Holy Spirit, and ask Him to shine His bright light into your heart so you won't just do good things, but do good things for the right reason.

Can you remember something you did that you thought was right, but it turned out to be awful? What happened?

How do you feel when you see a friend about to make a huge mistake and you want to warn them? Do you say anything? Why or why not?

What is your definition of selfishness? Do you ever think you fit that definition? Explain.

DAY 4

A person's spirit can endure sickness, but who can survive a broken spirit? —Proverbs 18:14

What do you think of when you hear the phrase "a hard heart"? I think of criminals in the movies who have been behind bars for decades and look like they want to kill someone. Or I think of the mug shots of serial killers I see on TV. But that's not actually the essence of a hard heart.

Remember how Proverbs 4:23 says we should guard our hearts above all things because all the issues of life flow from our hearts? Having a hard heart simply means we begin to close ourselves off to the voice of God or the voices of our brothers and sisters in Christ.

Our hearts grow hard in different ways. The more we sin, the harder our hearts become. Not only that, but pain can also cause your heart to grow hard. Whether it's abuse, neglect, a bad relationship or severe disappointment, when we get hurt emotionally we tend to get defensive in our souls. It becomes more difficult to trust others and even to trust God. So we slowly harden our hearts as a way to defend against getting hurt again.

The warning from this verse is this: Trouble awaits those of us who harden our hearts. When we stop feeling the loving conviction of the Spirit and stop caring about disobeying God's commands, the end result is always pain and trouble.

You can avoid that negative result by keeping your heart soft and open to Jesus. Worship Him. Talk to Him. Listen to Him. Get alone with Him. Ask Him to keep your heart soft and tender.

Give your own definition of a "hard heart."

Do you know anyone who seems to have a hard heart? What makes you think this?

What things do you harden your heart to? Be specific.

RELATIONSHIPS

SESSION FOUR

START

If there is one consistent area where people of all ages need wisdom, it's relationships. Relationships are central to who we are as human beings. After all, God intended us to be a growing, multiplying community of people who bring glory to Him in our relationships. But we all know relationships can be messy. The sin we bring into our relationships wreaks havoc on the way we interact with one another, which is why we desperately need God's wisdom when it comes to our relationships. Wisdom will not only help us see how important right relationships are to our growth as Christians, but also how to best navigate the relationships in our lives for both our good and God's glory.

WATCH

Fill in the blanks to follow along as you watch the Session 4 video.

1. God hardwired us for __Relationships__ with people.

2. __Wisdom__ itself is that friend you should pursue a relationship with.

3. God has created us to __Need__ each other and to __lean__ on each other.

4. The way God chooses to __take care__ of His kids is by __using__ His kids to __take Care__ of His kids.

5. We __need__ each other, and there is no way to __avoid__ that.

Discuss

1. What relationships in your life could benefit from wisdom right now?

2. How has this session's video challenged you when it comes to thinking about the importance of wisdom in navigating life's relationships?

James 2:6

GROUP DISCUSSION

The majority of this session will teach us wisdom from Proverbs and James about the importance of relationships within our lives. But before we dive into these two books' wisdom on relationships, let's first go back to the beginning—where relationships all started.

Read Genesis 1:26-27.

> *Then God said, "Let us make man in our image, according to our likeness. They will rule the fish of the sea, the birds of the sky, the livestock, the whole earth, and the creatures that crawl on the earth." So God created man in his own image; he created him in the image of God; he created them male and female.* —Genesis 1:26-27

The first and most important relationship human beings have is with God. God created us in His image so we would know and love Him and reflect His glory and beauty throughout our lives. One of the ways we reflect His glory and beauty in our lives is by rightly relating to others.

In what ways does your life show that your relationship with God is your top priority?

Why should your relationship with God come before relationships with your boyfriend/girlfriend, friends, and even family members?

While our relationship with God should always be our first priority, it is important to recognize that God didn't create us to be alone with Him. He created us to relate to one another. Self-sacrificing, other-centered love is at the heart of all meaningful relationships. As Genesis 1:27 tells us, both men and women are created in God's image and given the task to rule and reign over creation.

Why do you God hardwired us as social beings? How does this reflect Him?

God created us to be in relationship with Him and others. But at the center of our relationships with others, God created a unique relationship that serves as the fundamental building block of society and culture—the marriage relationship. This relationship exists between one man and one woman for life.

Read Genesis 1:28.

> *God blessed them, and God said to them, "Be fruitful, multiply, fill the earth, and subdue it. Rule the fish of the sea, the birds of the sky, and every creature that crawls on the earth." –Genesis 1:28*

God designed the marriage relationship between a husband and a wife as a lifetime commitment to each other both for His glory and our good and joy. This is the most unique relationship we can experience; it is designed to illustrate some pretty important truths about God and His relationship with His children.

In Ephesians 5, Paul compared a man's love of his wife to the way Christ leads and loves the church—sacrificially loving, serving, and laying down His life for her (vv. 25-31,33). He compared a woman's attitude to her husband to the way Christ obeyed and submitted to His Father's will (vv. 22-24,33). In Christian marriage, there is no room for selfish, self-seeking, and demanding behavior. Marriage is about reflecting God and His goodness as one person loves and serves the other.

While the marriage relationship is unique and reflective of God's relationship with us, it isn't the only relationship that should be marked by love and selflessness. Our friendship should be characterized by a similar selflessness and care.

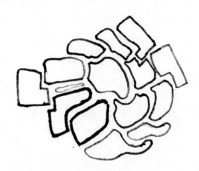

Do not owe anyone anything, except to love one another, for the one who loves another has fulfilled the law. The commandments, Do not commit adultery; do not murder; do not steal; do not covet; and any other commandment, are summed up by this commandment: Love your neighbor as yourself. Love does no wrong to a neighbor. Love, therefore, is the fulfillment of the law. —Romans 13:8-10

In which of your relationships do you see your selfishness the most?

Why do you think love is the basis of all healthy relationships?

How different do you think marriages, families, churches, neighborhoods, cities, and nations would look if we all lived out this wonderful commandment?

Think about Jesus' friendships for a second. From a worldly perspective, think about how inconvenient His friendships were. His friendships with sinners made Him scandalous, His disciples messed up a lot and seemed to often misunderstand Him. In His darkest hour, Jesus was even abandoned by those who were closest to Him.

Why is it wrong to pursue friendships only because of what you can get out of them?

Despite all of these things, Jesus still sought out these friends, inviting them into His life and ministry. Unlike so many of us, Jesus saw relationships as ends in themselves, not as a means to an end. In other words, He never befriended someone because of what that person could do for Him. Instead, He welcomed people who had nothing to offer and gave freely of Himself.

As image-bearers, we're called to reflect the God who made us. God has loved the world and loved us with a transforming, life-giving love. This love—reflected through His people—is more than a warm and fuzzy feeling, and it certainly isn't the kind of intoxicating infatuation in most romance stories. It's a transforming power, deeply affecting all it touches, changing it for the better.

How can you better reflect God in your relationships with others this week?

PERSONAL STUDY

DAY 1

There are four guidelines for relationships found in the wisdom literature of Proverbs. If you apply them to your dating relationships, and ultimately in your marriage, you will have a much better chance of enjoying a lifetime of intimacy and friendship with your husband or wife. Consider these four principals before you get romantically involved with someone, and especially before you choose to marry the person you one day fall in love with.

1. DON'T DATE ANYONE YOU WOULDN'T WANT TO MARRY.

> *She makes her own bed coverings; her clothing is fine linen and purple. … Strength and honor are her clothing, and she can laugh at the time to come. Her mouth speaks wisdom, and loving instruction is on her tongue.* –Proverbs 31:22,25-26

Look at the kind of people this verse describes. They are respected, honored, strong, wise, able to teach and instruct, and full of dignity. These are beautiful qualities each of us should strive for in our own lives, as well as the kind of relationships we want to be in.

Beyond your friendships, set your standards high and decide what kind of person you want to spend the rest of your life with. Once you've made a list of the qualities you want this person to embody, do not compromise in your dating life. Remember every date is a potential mate. You could easily fall in love with someone who would make a fun boyfriend but a horrible husband. These verses paint a picture of a husband and a wife who are wise, respected, strong, and prepared for the future. This is the kind of marriage we should all pray for. But do more than pray for it—prepare for it.

Do you have clear standards for the kind of person you want to marry one day? If so, what are they?

Take a minute to write out your standards for the kind of person you are willing to date, as well as the kind of person you will not go out with.

What older people have the freedom to speak into your life in the area of your relationships?

DAY 2.

2. DON'T DATE JUST FOR FUN: HAVE A PURPOSE AND A PLAN.

Who can find a wife of noble character? She is far more precious than jewels. —Proverbs 31:10

We've heard students say for years that there just aren't any good guys or girls to choose from when it comes to dating. Maybe the reason there are so many dating websites and smart phone apps is because single people feel like they just can't find any good people they'd be willing to date or marry.

You can hear this sentiment echoed in this verse that asks the basic question, "Who can find a good guy or girl these days?" This verse applies to guys and girls. You should date for the purpose of finding a spouse, and you should search for a spouse with personal integrity, conviction, a growing love for Jesus, and noble character. They are tough to find, but not impossible—so start now.

When you're young, relationships are supposed to be fun! So have a good time, but do it with your friends. Don't find all of your fun in a romantic relationship as a teenager, because what starts off as fun ends up in a fight, and before you know it your dating life is more dramatic than a show on a TV drama.

Marriage is the place where God will use another person to support, love, encourage, and sharpen you. This verses says the goal is for your hearts to fully trust each other and for neither of you to lack anything that you need. That sounds like a great way to live, and trust us when we tell you—it really is!

Have you ever dated someone? If so, what kind of relationship was it or what kind of relationship is it?

What kinds of questions do you plan to ask yourself before you get in a committed relationship with another person?

If a good wife (or husband) has more value than precious jewels, how important do you think it is for you to have a plan and a set of standards for the kind of person you're seeking out for marriage?

DAY 3.

3. GUARD YOUR EYES AND YOUR HEART.

Don't lust in your heart for her beauty or let her captivate you with her eyelashes. —Proverbs 6:25

Proverbs is full of warnings about what happens when we are seduced by the promise of sexual pleasure from outside the context of marriage. Specifically, this verse fits in a larger context of avoiding what is called "the adulteress." The warning, however, applies to any kind of sexual seduction that appeals to the eyes and the heart. At first it seems harmless. But if you allow the desire to grow stronger and stronger, eventually giving in, it will cost you more than you ever dreamed. It's better to guard your eyes and not even glance toward sinful relationships, because what enters through your eyes lands in your heart.

This wisdom can be applied to lust, pornography, a TV show with graphic sexual scenes, or even going online to find an ex- boyfriend or girlfriend on social media just to "see what they're doing now." Remember the wisdom of Proverbs 4:23,

"Guard your heart above all else, for it is the source of life." Guarding our eyes and our hearts is clearly an essential part of having healthy relationships.

Have you allowed certain things to enter your heart through the portal of your eyes that don't need to be there?

Do you have standards for what you will and will not watch on a TV show or in a movie? Why or why not?

Do you struggle with lust or impure thoughts? If so, could there be something you're doing or watching that feeds that lust and makes it grow?

DAY 4

4. AVOID TEMPTATION BY EMBRACING WISDOM.

She will keep you from a forbidden woman, a wayward woman with her flattering talk. —Proverbs 7:5

The best way to resist temptation is to simply avoid it, and the best way to avoid it is to embrace wisdom. If you pursue relationships for the purpose of your own pleasure, you will be lured into sexual sin because sin is always fun for a season. After the short, momentary pleasure has passed, there is a much longer season that can be filled with shame, regret, and consequences. If you pursue wisdom, you will walk a path that leads you away from tempting words, images, fantasies, and destructive relationships.

This verse makes a promise. If you ask for and pursue wisdom, you can avoid the consequences of a bad relationship that's personified here as "a wayward woman with her flattering talk." This sounds a lot like flirting, doesn't it? But what can seem like a little harmless flirting can lead to big problems. Clayton and I were friends with a couple for several years before their marriage ended in divorce and their kids were devastated by the breakup. The reason? One of their parents began flirting around with a co-worker. What started as something seemingly harmless ended up affecting numerous people, including children who never saw the divorce coming.

Are you getting too close to certain people who may drag you away from Christ or cause you to compromise in certain areas of your life?

Have you ever allowed friends to influence you to drink, party, lie to your parents, or go places you know you shouldn't go?

Make a list of all your friends who encourage you to live a holy life. Then make a list of your friends that are a negative influence on you. Which list is longer?

ACTIONS AND ATTITUDES

START

The Bible has a lot to say about our actions and attitudes, especially when those actions stem from an attitude of either pride or humility. God sees pride as the essence of every other sin. At its most basic level, pride is ultimately about self-worship since it seeks to place oneself on the throne in place of God. Humility, is the opposite of pride. It recognizes God's rightful place on the throne of our hearts, which is ultimately reflected in the selfless way we live toward others.

In this session, we will see how these two opposites—pride and humility—are contrasted with each other, and how one is the path toward wisdom and the other to destruction.

WATCH

Fill in the blanks to follow along as you watch the Session 5 video.

1. Pride is an attitude of _____; it's a perspective we have of ourselves that _____ us above where we belong.

2. Our _____ always precedes our _____.

3. When you are _____ enough to place God in the center of your life instead of yourself, your heart and mind are not _____ with your own selfish desires.

4. You can walk away from the crippling weight of _____, and you can enjoy letting the Holy Spirit have _____ of your life.

5. Humbling ourselves is simply _____ ourselves completely to God.

6. A right _____ leads to right _____.

Discuss

1. Why do think humility doesn't come naturally to us as humans?

2. How has this session's video challenged you when it comes to thinking about humility in your own life?

GROUP DISCUSSION

Pride is the opposite of humility, but let's spend some time exploring what the Bible has to say about pride. Only with a clearer picture of the devastating nature of pride within our hearts will we sense our desperate need for true humility.

We see the monstrous nature of pride from the very first pages of Scripture.

Read Genesis 3:5.

> *"In fact, God knows that when you eat it your eyes will be opened and you will be like God, knowing good and evil."* –Genesis 3:5

The crazy thing about what took place in this narrative is this: Adam and Eve already possessed glory given to them by God. They were created in God's image, and as a result, they reflected the glory of their Creator. However, at some point during this temptation, they wanted the Creator's glory too. They wanted to be like God, denying their dependence upon Him and attempting to declare for themselves what is good.

How does pride show itself in your own relationships?

Pride devours everything in its path, seeking its own satisfaction, its own centrality, and its own glory. Whether in the subtle desire to have what someone else has or the overwhelming self-obsession we see on social media, pride is everywhere. You don't have to be loud and obnoxious to be prideful—sometimes it shows up in selfish solitude, silently judging others, or in the privacy of our own thoughts.

In essence, pride is shorthand for self-worship, and self-worship is in the DNA of every other sin. Pride is the root sin from which all other sins come.

Make a list of common sins. How can these sins be traced back to the root of pride?

So now that we've seen what lies at the heart of all sin, let's go back and look at humanity's original sin in context.

Read Genesis 3:1-6.

> *Now the serpent was the most cunning of all the wild animals that the Lord God had made. He said to the woman, "Did God really say, 'You can't eat from any tree in the garden'?" The woman said to the serpent, "We may eat the fruit from the trees in the garden. But about the fruit of the tree in the middle of the garden, God said, 'You must not eat it or touch it, or you will die.'"*

> *"No! You will not die," the serpent said to the woman. "In fact, God knows that when you eat it your eyes will be opened and you will be like God, knowing good and evil." The woman saw that the tree was good for food and delightful to look at, and that it was desirable for obtaining wisdom. So she took some of its fruit and ate it; she also gave some to her husband, who was with her, and he ate it.* –Genesis 3:1-6

This passage shows us that behavior problems are belief problems. Eve opted to disbelieve God's promise and to disobey. She chose to believe in herself and her own version of what is good rather than believing in God and what He knows to be truly good.

Notice the three-pronged promises to sin Eve experienced:

- It is satisfying (if only temporarily)

- It is pretty

- It is enlightening

Where do we look to find satisfaction, beauty, and enlightenment?

The promises that fed Eve's pride feed the pride within our own hearts. We disobey God because we believe the lies that something will satisfy more than He does, something is more beautiful that He is, and that whatever this something is, it is something we deserve.

But here's the sad news: When we place ourselves at the center of the universe, everything goes wrong. The result of Adam and Eve's disobedience was creation gone astray. All of the relationships God created were broken—humanity's relationship with God, humanity's relationship with each other, and humanity's relationship with creation. Much like the chaos, disaster, and death that would come if we were to knock our sun from the center of our solar system, the removal of God from the center of Adam and Eve's hearts created its own devastation.

> **Think of the most recent conflict you've had with someone close to you (friend, teacher, coach, family member, etc.). How did pride contribute to the conflict?**

So if pride is a the root of all of our sin, and if we are all infected with hearts of selfish pride, then what do we do? What hope do we have?

In short, we need a heart change. If the problem is a pride issue deep within our heats, then we need Someone powerful enough to get to the root and change us from within.

Read Matthew 4:1-11.

> *Then Jesus was led up by the Spirit into the wilderness to be tempted by the devil. After he had fasted forty days and forty nights, he was hungry. Then the tempter approached him and said, "If you are the Son of God, tell these stones to become bread." He answered, "It is written: Man must not live on bread alone but on every word that comes from the mouth of God." Then the devil took him to the holy city, had him stand on the pinnacle of the temple, and said to him, "If you are the Son of God, throw yourself down. For it is written: He will give his angels orders concerning you, and they will support you with their hands so that you will not strike your foot against a stone." Jesus told him, "It is also written: Do not test the Lord your God." Again, the devil took him to a very high mountain and showed him all the kingdoms of the world and their splendor. And he said to him, "I will give you all these things if you will fall down and worship me." Then Jesus told him, "Go away, Satan! For it is written: Worship the Lord your God, and serve only him." Then the devil left him, and angels came and began to serve him.* –Matthew 4:1-11

Compare Jesus' wilderness temptation to Eve's temptation in the garden. How are the three desires of pride expressed in both stories?

What can we learn about fighting our own temptations by looking at how Jesus successfully fought against His?

The narrative of Jesus' temptation shows us that the total redemption available to us is through Jesus' work, not ours. Where Adam and Eve failed, Jesus came through. Where we failed, He succeeded. We are sinful through and through, filled with all kinds of pride and selfishness. But Jesus is sinless, and His sacrifice on our behalf is the good news for getting our hearts cleansed from the stain of pride we all know too well. The real power to fight pride and be humble isn't found within us at all—it's Jesus. The real power lies with the one who killed pride through His sinless life, sacrifice on the cross, and resurrection from the dead. The One who also happens to be willing to change your heart if you ask Him.

How can we cultivate better awareness of pride in our lives? What should our response when we see it?

PERSONAL STUDY

DAY 1

He mocks those who mock, but gives grace to the humble. The wise will inherit honor, but he holds up fools to dishonor. –Proverbs 3:34-35

Do you want to pour our His grace on your life? Do you want Him to notice your life and how you live? Then choose humility. Do you want God to oppose you? Do you want to experience embarrassment and shame? Then choose pride and arrogance. Humility brings God's favor. Arrogance brings shame.

We've seen this over and over and over again. In all our years of ministry, we have noticed that when pastors and leaders get caught in a secret sin, they never end up fully repenting and experiencing restoration. But when a pastor or leader confesses their secret sin, they almost always end up going through a process of reconciliation. What is the difference? One is caught while the other one confesses. The one who is caught usually reacts in pride and arrogance. The one who confesses responds in humility and submission. The result is simple. The attitude of pride leads to a defensive posture that refuses to submit to God or others, to any kind of accountability or attempts to correct sinful behavior. The attitude of humility that led the leaders to confess before they got caught carries them through a season of learning, repenting, growing, and eventually being restored in their relationships (though not necessarily to their former position in leadership).

So when Scripture says God mocks proud mockers, it paints a picture of God issuing a warning to stubborn people who refuse to listen. Then when they go their own way and end up suffering the very things God warned them about, it is as if He shakes His head and says, "I tried my best to show you a better way, but you were too foolish to listen. You mocked my statutes, but you now see I was right."

When it comes to God's Word, you can break the rules. You just can't make the rules. God makes them and they are for your good and His glory.

How do you feel inside when other people mock you or make fun of you?

Can you remember a time when you made a foolish decision you later regretted?

What are some ways you could increase the flow of wisdom into your life?

DAY 2

But he gives greater grace. Therefore he says: God resists the proud, but gives grace to the humble. Therefore, submit to God. Resist the devil, and he will flee from you. Draw near to God, and he will draw near to you. Cleanse your hands, sinners, and purify your hearts, you double-minded. —James 4:6-8

Pride draws us toward the devil. Humility draws us close to God.

Satan loves pride. God hates it. When we act in arrogance or show ourselves to be too proud to submit to our parents or listen to those in authority over us, Satan sees an opportunity to exploit our pride and bring destruction in our lives. We must resist the schemes of the devil to temp us this way. He wants to convince you that you don't need any help. You don't need anyone telling you what to do. You are fine all by yourself—and your parents, teachers, pastor, and youth leaders are all idiots. He'll tell you that you're smarter than all of them. But remember that the devil is a liar.

God, on the other hand, loves humility. He hates pride. He knows pride destroys us. Because He loves us, He hates anything that would hurt us. That's why God hates pride. So, the way to get closer in your relationship with God is to resist the devil every time he tempts you to ignore the wisdom of others. As you resist the devil, you can move closer to God in humility. God will see how hard you're trying to avoid the enemy and run toward Him. God promises that, as you put forth the effort to pursue Him, He will come your way and meet you there. This is a promise He keeps every time.

What does "drawing near to God" look like for you?

So you struggle with resisting the devil when he comes at you with temptation. What are the primary ways he tempts you?

What areas of your life have you not fully submitted to God?

DAY 3

A fool's way is right in his own eyes, but whoever listens to counsel is wise. —Proverbs 12:15

It takes real humility to do these two very important things: listen to advice and overlook an insult.

In order to listen to advice from someone else, you have to admit that the other person knows something you don't know. The action of listening first requires the attitude of humility. To overlook an insult, you have to admit you are not so important that you can't forgive someone for hurting your feelings, because your feelings are not the ultimate thing in your life. The ability to overlook an insult results from an attitude of internal humility.

One way you can practically overlook the insults of others is to ask yourself why you take it to heart when you are insulted. The reason it stings so bad could possibly reveal your insecurity. People who are completely grounded in the love of Jesus are less likely to get bent out of shape when someone says something hurtful to them. When you know you have nothing to prove and allow what God thinks about you to define you, you are not worried about what other people think about you.

However, it's more difficult to let an insult go if you base your self worth on what you believe other people think about you. So many times we fall into the habit of allowing other people's opinions of us define how we act, how we dress, who our friends are and who we date. But we should only let the gospel define us. When we do, we are liberated to quit trying to please others and stop feeling the need to defend ourselves when we are insulted or when someone talks trash about us.

Can you name three people that you regularly seek out for wisdom? If you can't, make a list with names of some wise people and commit to asking them if they would be willing to mentor you.

How do you usually react when you feel like someone has insulted you, either to your face or behind your back?

Do you find yourself looking online or on social media to see what other people think about you based on likes, follows, or comments?

DAY 4

When people first saw John, they misunderstood who he was. This happened to me once.

I was in my late 20s and I was coming home from an event with FCA (Fellowship of Christian Athletes). I had been preaching at the event. I also led worship all weekend, so I had my guitar with me.

I was in the airport in Nashville, Tennessee. It's the Country Music capital of the world, and I was carrying a guitar. Do you see where this is going?

I walked out of the restroom and what happened next is one of my favorite stories. A girl and her boyfriend saw me, made a crazy surprise face, then ran at me. The girl squealed. The boy just stared. Then she spoke to me as she hyper-ventilated and fanned her face. "Oh my gosh! I cannot believe it's you! I love you! We both love you so much!

Seriously. I had no clue who she thought I was. This had never happened to me before, but I assumed she had me confused with someone famous. Since it was

Nashville and I was carrying a guitar, I figured she thought I was a country music star. So I decided to see how things played out, hoping she would finally tell me who she thought I was.

She continued. "Can I have your autograph?" She handed me a piece of paper, a receipt or something, and fumbled around to find a pen. I didn't know what name to write on the paper! I didn't want to sign somebody else's name, and even if I did, I didn't know who to sign because I still didn't know who she thought I was. So I decided to write my own name. But I signed it really fast and sloppy, like a famous person would do, and I handed it back to her. She stared at if for a second then looked back at me and said, "This is the best thing ever! I have all your records. I've seen you in concert twice. Every time I hear 'Unanswered Prayers' it makes me want to cry. My family is never going to believe I met Garth Brooks!"

It's so easy for us to misunderstand who a person is, even the people we know. When people thought John was the Messiah, he made sure to set them straight. He died to pride and embraced humility. He pointed them away from him and toward the real Savior, Jesus Christ. May we always do the same.

When do you enjoy being recognized by other people? When do you not enjoy being recognized by other people? Explain.

How does it make you feel when other people notice you?

Talk about one thing that has happened in your life that God used to create humility in your heart.

START

Some of you may have never worked a day in your life beyond doing household chores. But here's a fact: You will have a job at some point. Maybe in the near future you'll work in a part-time job mowing lawns or lifeguarding during the summers, but eventually you'll get to a place in life where you have to start earning some income for yourself. Even though your first job (or two) might not be your dream job, the fact that you are working is a good thing in itself.

God designed work, and like everything else God designed—it is *good*. Work is one more way we get to reflect God and serve others. But the good gift of work was distorted because of the fall. Because of that, we have wrong attitudes and perceptions when it comes to the task of work. But because of the gospel—Jesus' work on our behalf—our work once again becomes purposeful. Our work points back to the way God originally designed things and forward to the new creation.

WATCH

Fill in the blanks to follow along as you watch the Session 6 video.

1. Work is actually a _____ and it was God's _____ from the very beginning.

2. The Bible shows us that work teaches us _____ and _____.

3. Laziness is always associated with _____ in the Bible, but hard work is always connected to _____.

4. It's our job as Christians to _____ _____, with the power of the Holy Spirit, so that people can have their _____ met.

Discuss

1. How does our culture view work? Is you idea and attitude toward work reflective of the cultural attitude?

2. How has this session challenged you when it comes to thinking about the Bible's perspective on work?

Answers: 1) blessing, idea; 2) patience, perseverance; 3) fools, wisdom; 4) work hard, needs

GROUP DISCUSSION

When we imagine the garden of Eden—in books, paintings, or movies—there seems to be a lot of lounging around. Adam and Eve are reclining, relaxing, and eating grapes as lions and lambs lay nearby. It looks like the ultimate vacation spot, equipped with the best orchards and vineyards.

> **Why do you think the pop culture perspective of Eden is a place of rest and relaxation, not of work?**

The funny thing is, this image of Eden is completely of our own creation, and not the image that is portrayed in the Bible. The Bible doesn't talk about Eden as being a perpetual day spa with hot spring baths, massages, and smoothies. Instead, it was an active community where Adam and Eve had work to do and showed up to do it six days a week. Far from the negative attitude toward work in our culture, the Bible presents work as something created by God, and designed to be good for humans.

Read Genesis 2:15-17.

> *The LORD God took the man and placed him in the garden of Eden to work it and watch over it. And the LORD God commanded the man, "You are free to eat from any tree of the garden, but you must not eat from the tree of the knowledge of good and evil, for on the day you eat from it, you will certainly die." –Genesis 2:15-17*

The garden was a workplace. Adam was at work in verse 19, naming the animals. In the same way that God had taken the chaos and void of creation and brought order, mankind was meant to continue the work by tending the garden, naming the animals, and caring for and expanding the order and beauty of God's world. Adam's work was a good thing. It tells us we were made to work, collaborating with God's creative work, care-taking, nurturing, and developing.

Do you think of school as work? Why or why not? What are some other places besides school where we make order out of chaos?

How does our culture demean and diminish the value of work?

The Bible is clear that work is a good thing, but because of sin, it is often a struggle. Ever since sin entered the world, what was meant for our good has been cursed, and our efforts in work push against a world that resists us. We looked at God's intention for human effort in the garden in Genesis 2. Now let's look further to see what happened after the fall.

Read Genesis 3:17-19.

> *And he said to the man, "Because you listened to your wife and ate from the tree about which I commanded you, 'Do not eat from it': The ground is cursed because of you. You will eat from it by means of painful labor all the days of your life. It will produce thorns and thistles for you, and you will eat the plants of the field. You will eat bread by the sweat of your brow until you return to the ground, since you were taken from it. For you are dust, and you will return to dust." –Genesis 3:17-19*

Do you see what happened? Work was created as a collaboration with God, done in harmony with the world around us, but it suddenly became an uphill battle. The soil braced itself against us, weeds crept into our gardens, and the branches that produced food grew thorns.

Because of the fall, we usually sin in our work one of two ways. The first is when we let work define us. Allowing our work to define us makes it an idol. When that happens, our whole lives are spent in service to it, sacrificing relationships, family, and health and well-being for its sake.

Some of you may love doing schoolwork, a sport or hobby, or something other skill you have. Discuss how you would feel if your ability to do it any longer was taken away. How would you respond?

How do we fight the temptation to allow our performance to define us?

While work is certainly a good thing, it is only fulfilling when it's experienced in the context of a relationship with God. In that relationship, work is a way of participating in what God is doing in the world.

The other way the fall has made our work go off the rails is when we let work overwhelm us to the point of exhaustion. When this happens, work becomes the "daily grind" or a chore to get through, a source of emotional exhaustion. But we can only find ourselves in such a place when we've lost sight of the Creator. Apart from Him, we can't see the bigger purpose our work might serve in creation. We can't see that our role—however small it seems—is good.

When was the last time work left you feeling overwhelmed? Or when did work feel futile and pointless?

What got you through it? How did you press on?

It is only through the gospel that the effects of the fall can be reversed when it comes to our work. The gospel itself—the work of Jesus in His life, death, and resurrection—is a work that frees us from the exhausting effects of work. Because of Jesus' work, we also have hope for what work will look like in the future. Thorns and thistles might dominate our landscape today, but a day is coming when they won't be a problem for us.

The apostle John gave us a glimpse of that world in the Book of Revelation.

Read Revelation 21:22–22:5.

> *I did not see a temple in it, because the Lord God the Almighty and the Lamb are its temple. The city does not need the sun or the moon to shine on it, because the glory of God illuminates it, and its lamp is the Lamb. The nations will walk by its light, and the kings of the earth will bring their glory into it. Its gates will never close by day because it will never be night there. They will bring the glory and honor of the nations into it. Nothing unclean will ever enter it, nor anyone who does what is detestable or false, but only those written in the Lamb's book of life. Then he showed me the river of the water of life, clear as crystal, flowing from the throne of God and of the Lamb down the middle of the city's main street. The tree of life was on each side of the river, bearing twelve kinds of fruit, producing its fruit every month. The leaves of the tree are for healing the nations, and there will no longer be any curse. The throne of God and of the Lamb will be in the city, and his servants will worship him. They will see his face, and his name will be on their foreheads. Night will be no more; people will not need the light of a lamp or the light of the sun, because the Lord God will give them light, and they will reign forever and ever.* –Revelation 21:22–22:5*

Until that day comes, we can only catch glimpses of it. We do so as we work for the good of our schools, cities, and neighborhoods, and serving others. Our lives show that work is good, but it isn't everything.

PERSONAL STUDY

DAY 1

For just as the body without the spirit is dead, so also faith without works is dead. –James 2:26

Take a few minutes to read James 2:14-16. Notice the importance James placed on our good works and how our good works flow from our faith in Jesus. According to James, our good deeds do not save us, but they prove we have been saved. Now, think about the image he painted for us in verse 26. It's a bit unsettling. He said if we have faith in Jesus without any good works, it's the same thing as a dead body. There's a corpse but no life; a body without a spirit.

I don't know about you, but I've seen a lot of dead bodies in my life. As a pastor, I've preached a lot of funerals. I will never forget closing the casket on my father's dead body just moments before I preached his funeral on Father's Day in 2012. I knew that the corpse in that casket was not really my dad. Without a heartbeat, without breath in his lungs, without a mind that worked—it was just a shell of Joe King. This is how God sees us when we claim to be Christians but don't back it up with the way we live. The things we do, the way we love people, and the way we treat others is hard work, but those very things prove we've truly been saved and born again by believing the gospel of Jesus Christ.

People are not attracted to corpses. The only reason people gather around dead bodies is to pay respects at a funeral. People are drawn to life. Tens of thousands of fans will gather in stadiums to watch athletes compete in the Olympics, a soccer match, or a football game. Why? Because those athletes are doing work. They're moving. They have life. People are drawn to life giving atmospheres. When we work for the glory of God, people are drawn to us because of the life of Christ in us.

Do you consider yourself a natural worker or more wired to be a slacker? Why do you think that about yourself?

Do you usually take responsibility for things or do you sometimes blame others or make excuses? Give a few examples.

If you were put on trial for being a Christian, would there be enough evidence from your good works to convict you of actually being a follower of Jesus?

DAY 2

Know well the condition of your flock, and pay attention to your herds, for wealth is not forever; not even a crown lasts for all time.
—Proverbs 27:23-24

In the days of the Old Testament, a verse like this one had more significance than just spiritual encouragement for your relationship with God. This kind of advice literally meant the difference between living through the winter or dying when there was nothing to eat, nothing to wear, and nothing to burn to keep the family warm at night. For most of human history, and for much of the world's population today, the difference between survival and death is how hard families are willing to work for food, shelter, clothing, water, and basic needs.

Maybe you have never had to live like this, day to day, wondering if you will have food to eat or water to drink—but the principle still applies. In that context, all the wealth and possessions, lifestyle, and survival of a family depended on the family paying attention to the condition of it's livestock, because that's where they got meat, milk, butter, and wool. They used their livestock to trade for other items they needed to live. The lesson here is simple; we must do the hard work of taking care of what God has entrusted to us. When we manage small things well, God will entrust us with bigger things. Our hard work pays off in the long run, but laziness leads to regret and shame.

Wealth doesn't last forever. I remember the stock market crash of 2008. For the next six years, the world economy was in what experts called "The Great Recession." Home values plummeted and the unemployment rate rose to almost

9 percent. People were panicking all over the planet, but my dad said something very wise. He said as long as you know how to work, and you're not spending more money than you make, you will be fine. That's the heart of this verse and the wisdom of paying attention to your work ethic.

Do you have a job and make any kind of income? Explain.

Do you tithe and give to your church off of the money you make? Why or why not?

Describe what you do to stay on top of your finances, your schedule, and all your personal responsibilities.

What are some ways you could "pay attention to your herds" better?

DAY 3

The one who works his land will have plenty of food, but whoever chases fantasies will have his fill of poverty. —Proverbs 28:19

Work carries it's own benefits with it. I can remember how it felt every single Friday at five in the evening during my summers growing up. All the men would punch a time card, and as they were walking out to the parking lot to leave for the weekend, they would walk through my dad's office. He owned the motor shop that they all worked in, and as they walked past his desk, he would hand them a paycheck. Then all those men would drive straight to the bank and deposit that money into their checking accounts so they could spend it however they needed to.

When they were all gone, it was just me and my dad. I would lock up the warehouse, we would walk out to his truck together, and he would drive us home. That's when he would hand me cash. It would be the amount of money he owed me for the work I'd done that week. Back then I got paid $5 an hour, so for a 40 hour work week, he would give me $200 cash. I was "working my land" back then and it felt so satisfying to get paid for that work. I'd set aside the first $20 for my tithe to the church, and I would stick the rest in an old cigar box in my bedroom, until I opened a checking account when I was 16. With that money, I saw this verse come true as I "had plenty of food." I could pay for my own car, my insurance, my own clothes and shoes, and even put some money aside for the future.

I had a friend named AJ. He spent all summer inside the house, in the air conditioning, watching TV. He always talked about how he would be rich one day because he was going to own his own business. He dreamed a lot. But they were just fantasies. He never worked at making his dreams a reality, and he never brought God any glory with the work he did.

Hard work doesn't make you better than lazy people, but it does place you in a position of blessing and favor that slackers will never experience.

List some things you are working on right now.

List some things you've slacked off on over the past year.

What are some dreams you have for your future? Write our your plan to achieve them.

DAY 4

Wealth obtained by fraud will dwindle, but whoever earns it through labor will multiply it. ... but the sinner's wealth is stored up for the righteous. –Proverbs 13:11,22

It is not a sin to have money. It's a sin for money to have you.

Numerous verses in Proverbs show us how we can handle money wisely, but money and wealth are always connected with hard work. This positive view of hard work is contrasted to a negative picture of people who get money in dishonest ways; usually by stealing, lying, or deceiving people. Any wealth you gain in any other way than hard work will one day disappear.

However, hard work over time will bring you wealth as long as you manage it wisely by saving it instead of spending it. This is not so much a lesson about money; it's a lesson about the eternal value of your work. Long after you are dead and gone, if you have worked hard and saved what you made, you will be able to provide an inheritance for your grandchildren.

Isn't it crazy to think that right now, as a young woman or young man, your work ethic will one day allow you to bless your kids and your grandkids in ways that will live on after you've died? This is why we said at the very beginning of this chapter that work is not a curse. It is a blessing from God, and when viewed correctly from Scripture, it's the best way to develop Godly character, humility, and a dependence of God to provide all your needs for a lifetime.

List a few areas of your life where you may tend to slack off and get lazy.

Are there things your parents are constantly asking you to do that you like to avoid or procrastinate in doing? What are those areas?

If we surveyed your friends, would they say you have a strong work ethic or would they say you're somewhat of a slacker?

MONEY
AND STUFF

START

It's sort of crazy to think about the various hobbies and collectibles people invest their time and income toward. For some people, every extra dollar they make goes into buying and collecting the latest pair of Jordan's. Others buy every collectible item associated with a particular favorite movie franchise, like *Jurassic Park, Harry Potter,* or *The Avengers*. There are as many different areas to collect "things" and invest in "things" as there are people. The adage "one man's trash is another man's treasure" in this case couldn't be more true.

Behind our hobbies and collectibles, or whatever we spend our money on, lies a deeper philosophy of how we view money and the things invest in. Like all matters of life, the Bible wants us to think deeply about how we should see money (and stuff), recognizing the sometimes hidden motivations within our hearts when it comes to how we handle money in our own lives.

WATCH

Fill in the blanks to follow along as you watch the Session 7 video.

1. Your own heart will be *refreshed* when you see how good it feels to give away your money and your stuff to *help others*.

2. When you *bless* others, you receive a *greater* blessing.

3. Nothing is truly *ours*. All that you have is on *loan* from God.

4. It's not *money* we should pursue—it's *righteousness*.

5. When you are *grounded*, you will *grow*.

Discuss

1. How does our attitude toward money and our possessions reflect what we are deeply passionate about?

2. How has this session's video challenged you when it comes to thinking about money and possessions?

GROUP DISCUSSION

Have you ever heard the name Elanor Boyer? Chances are, probably not. Back in 1997, Elanor Boyer, at the time 72 years old, hit the lottery jackpot and collected $11.8 million dollars.

What would you do with that amount of money? What do you think Ms. Boyer did?

Ms. Boyer was a Christian. She whole-heartedly believed that God had always taken cared of her. Because of that, Ms. Boyer felt completely comfortable giving away *all* of her winnings. She gave the money to her church and to various groups serving the town where she grew up. According to Ms. Boyer, "No new car, no vacation. My life is no different. I've given it up to God. I live in His presence and do His will, and I did that from the start."[1]

It's one thing to say you believe something, but it's something entirely different to live out that belief. Think about it: We all have stated beliefs. We say we believe this or that, but sometimes the way we actually live contradicts what we say we believe. We actually do the very opposite of what we say we believe. We say we believe all life is sacred and valued but we are completely silent it comes to defending the rights of the unborn or an oppressed minority group. Or we say we believe sharing the gospel is absolutely necessary for our friends to know Christ but we never take an opportunity to talk about Jesus with them. When contradictions like this happen, the way we live or our actions actually have a way of revealing what we truly believe. We say we believe something, but our actions say otherwise.

What are some stated beliefs you have that you have found difficulty living out? Explain why?

How does Ms. Boyer's stated belief match up to her choice to give away her winnings? How do her actions challenge/inspire you?

Materialism and consumerism are two of the most popular worldviews. Materialism and consumerism say life and the way to a good life is all about having the latest and greatest toys. It is the promise of nearly every SUV and truck commercial. These commercials have someone going on an off-road adventure, to the summit of some remote mountain, or maybe winding down a sandy beach with a surfboard in tow. Whatever the setting, they don't want you to buy the car or jeep or truck being advertised—they want you to buy the lifestyle. They want you to buy into the idea experiences and "toys" like this are essential to your happiness in life.

What other commercials or products try to get you to buy into a certain lifestyle?

How often have you thought to yourself, "If only I could get this, then I would be happy?" Did it work? How long did the feeling last before you had the same thought about something else?

Read 1 Timothy 6:10.

For the love of money is a root of all kinds of evil, and by craving it, some have wandered away from the faith and pierced themselves with many griefs. —1 Timothy 6:10

Why is it important to emphasize money isn't the root of all kinds of evil, but rather the love of it?

Why do you think people fall in love with money itself?

There isn't any intrinsic value to money. The paper dollars or even the rare gems people want don't have any intrinsic worth to them. All of it is assigned worth from our society, so why fall in love with it?

The short answer is people don't necessarily love the money, but rather the things money can get them. They love wealth because they believe it can get them the things they think will make them happy. That wealth will offer the contentment and satisfaction that they so long for. But if we know anything about the history of some of the world's most wealthiest people, we know money can never deliver on this promise.

Read Hebrews 13:5.

> *Keep your life free from the love of money. Be satisfied with what you have, for he himself has said, I will never leave you or abandon you.*
> –Hebrews 13:5

Why did the author say we should be free from the love of money? Why is that significant?

The author of Hebrews makes it crystal clear that the way to be free from the love of money is to find greater satisfaction in knowing God is with us, and that He promises to never abandon us. Knowing this is true and living it out in our daily actions will make us into the type of people who won't find it difficult see and treat money as we should.

If people have money issues, it is because they have heart issues as well. Somewhere deep within is a dissatisfaction and discontentment. Until that is recognized and addressed, no amount of advice regarding money will make sense.

What have you learned about the Bible's teaching on money that has been eye-opening thus far?

What are some ways you can demonstrate with your life a greater love for God over any passion for possessions?

PERSONAL STUDY

DAY 1

When I was in middle school, the music world was taken by storm when MTV aired a music video called "Thriller." The artist was Michael Jackson and that record catapulted him to international fame unlike any other singer had ever known. Sony music estimates this record alone has sold over 100 million copies worldwide. It's also been certified Platinum 33 times and according to Billboard, "Thriller" is the biggest album of all time.[2] Obviously it made Michael Jackson rich beyond imagination.

He made over $500 million in his career. But would you believe that when he died tragically of a drug overdose, he was $500 million in debt? Would you believe that even though he sold over 750 million records over the course of his entire career, he had to declare bankruptcy in 2007 because he could not repay a $25 million loan?[3]

I remember watching the story unfold as the media continued to uncover more and more facts about his life; his bizarre behavior, his addiction to spending, and his struggle to cope with fame and fortune. The story was tragic and heartbreaking. Yet I also sense that God can teach us a lesson from all of this, and it's the simple truth that we should never tie our identity to our possessions, and our self worth is not equated with the stuff we own or the money we make. God alone can give us stability and satisfaction. No amount of money can ever buy you peace of mind. Don't spend your life chasing after something that doesn't exist. There is no true joy or real happiness apart from God.

List a few practical things you can learn from this story.

What can you do now to avoid this kind of tragic ending later?

Do you know anyone who has wealth but seems unhappy? How would you describe that person's life? What can you do to encourage that person?

DAY 2

I grew up in Fountain Inn, South Carolina. Our summers were sweltering. And because I grew up on a farm, I spent lots of time outdoors, especially in the summer, working in our fields and our garden. Things tend to grow when there's good sunlight, water, and soil. This is true for crops like tomatoes and corn and watermelons. It's also true for less desirable things, like kudzu.

You may have never heard of kudzu, but it's literally everywhere in the area where I grew up. It first came to America from Asia in the 1800s, but didn't become popular until 1935 when dust storms damaged farm land. Then, kudzu became the main weapon against soil erosion.[4] There was even a Kudzu Festival in Union, South Carolina when I was in high school. This plant climbs and coils and twists and is nearly impossible to kill. It has broad, green leaves and a root system that clings tight to the ground, burrowing deep into the soil. It's tough and tenacious.

If you want to grow, you need roots. If you want to be tough in the face of adversity and tenacious in the face of struggles, take a lesson from the kudzu weed. It's hard to kill and it grows fast on the surface because it has roots under the surface. Like Proverbs 11:28 says, "Anyone trusting in his riches will fail, but the righteous will flourish like foliage." The flourishing foliage of the kudzu plant can show us how righteousness leads to flourishing. On the other hand, you have a guaranteed way to fail. Just spend all your time trying to make more money and accumulate more stuff. There is no root in that life. It's a weak way to live and it can't sustain the pressures of life. You will wither up and die if you find your identity in your wealth or possessions, but you will flourish if you find them in Gods love for you.

What does it mean to you to be "grounded in God"?

Explain the meaning of the phrase, "When you are grounded, you will grow."

List some "spiritual roots" you can develop now to help you grow in wisdom.

DAY 3

Wealth is not profitable on a day of wrath, but righteousness rescues from death. —Proverbs 11:4

Robin Williams once said, "Cocaine is God's way of telling you that you are making too much money."[5] This is a strange thing to say, wouldn't you agree? And even though it came from the mouth of a comedian, it's not funny at all.

I laughed along with tens of millions of people who found Robin Williams hilarious in movies like *Mrs. Doubtfire* or even his TV show *Mork and Mindy*. Yet deep inside his own heart was a huge hole that could not be filled with drugs or alcohol—substances he struggled with throughout his career. Robin Williams was rich and famous. He got what so many people think they want, and those things alone were insufficient to bring him any peace on the inside. Tragically, he took his own life in his California home in 2014.

Let this be a wake up call for you. Wealth is not profitable (helpful, sufficient) when the really hard days of life come your way. In other words, money is not what gets you through the tough times. It cannot buy love, friendship, support, or encouragement. It cannot purchase the peace you are hard-wired to crave. Only a righteous life lived in a relationship with God can settle your restless heart. Pursuing righteousness in the fear of the Lord will rescue you from death, and not just physical death, in the ultimate resurrection from the dead. Pursuing righteousness will also save you from the spiritual and emotional death that plagues those who choose pleasure over God and worldly success over submission to Jesus as Lord.

All the money in the world was powerless to purchase one more day of life for Robin Williams, and it cannot bring you one moment of true, lasting joy. Money is not sinful, but it can cast a sinful spell on your soul as it competes for first place in your life. Wealth can never give you what God alone can provide.

What famous person do you know of who recently seemed to crash in public?

Would you rather have $10 million and no real friends, or make minimum wage but have three good friends you trusted? Why?

Why do you think so many celebrities (Elvis, Kurt Cobain, Robin Williams, Whitney Houston, Michael Jackson) die early and due to unnatural causes? What are they missing?

DAY 4

It is not a sin to have money. It's a sin for money to have you. Make no mistake, if you don't have a healthy, biblical view of wealth and possessions, you will get swept away by the tide of our culture, which is in essence all about getting all you can at the expense of others. Hard work is a blessing that can lead to financial security, but God's financial blessing on your life should lead to more than stability and security. It should lead to generosity. We are called to be generous not only toward our church (with our tithes and offerings) but also to others. There's a strong warning in Scripture for those who hoard all their money for themselves and refuse to treat others fairly or share their wealth with others.

> *Come now, you rich people, weep and wail over the miseries that are coming on you. Your wealth has rotted and your clothes are moth-eaten. Your gold and silver are corroded, and their corrosion will be a witness against you and will eat your flesh like fire. You have stored up treasure in the last days. Look! The pay that you withheld from the workers*

who mowed your fields cries out, and the outcry of the harvesters has reached the ears of the Lord of Hosts. You have lived luxuriously on the earth and have indulged yourselves. You have fattened your hearts in a day of slaughter. –James 5:1-5

James said those who live in luxury while ignoring others are storing up a treasure trove of pain and regret. Greed can cause you to take advantage of others, to turn a blind eye to justice, and will eventually leave you destitute. This Scripture tells us God is watching what we do with our money and what wealth does to our hearts.

The vaccine for greed is generosity. Generosity is not about getting the money out of your pockets. It's about getting the greed out of you heart. We are made in the image of a generous God who gave us His very best and most precious gift– His only Son. We can follow His example, by His Spirit, and choose generosity over greed.

When did you last give something away?

Do you tithe to your church? Why or why not?

Do you ever support ministries of missionaries? Explain.

Do you have a plan to set aside a percentage of any money you make to give it to God? If not, why not?

START

The things we say and the way we say them are pretty important, right? I think we all know this is true. We all know words have the amazing ability to build someone up and make their day, or completely ruin their day (or week) with an inappropriate joke or comment on social media. Words matter, and even more importantly, words mirror the heart attitudes within.

No matter how old you are, you need wisdom abut what to say and the words you use to say it. Thankfully, the Bible has a lot of wisdom on this topic, giving us clarity for how to live everyday life. Let's take a look at the wisdom behind words in our last week of study.

WATCH

Fill in the blanks to follow along as you watch the Session 8 video.

1. We can _____ people with the very words we say.

2. The goal is for us to become aware of the amazing _____ we have, and then we surrender that to Jesus for _____ purposes.

3. The way we use our words makes a difference in whether we are _____ in wisdom or not.

4. If you _____something good about someone, _____ it to them.

Discuss

1. Why do think humility doesn't come naturally to us as humans?

2. How has this session's video challenged you when it comes to thinking about humility in your own life?

Answers: 1) destroy; 2) gift, good; 3) grounded; 4) think, say

GROUP DISCUSSION

Words are powerful force to be used either for good or evil.

Recall a time when someone encouraged you by saying something positive about you. How did you respond? Why?

Now, think of a time when someone discouraged you by saying something negative about you. How did you respond? Why?

Why do you think words have the ability to make us feel either extremely encouraged or the complete opposite?

If words and speech are central to our everyday lives, and have the power to bring either encouragement or discouragement, then why do we often mess up in our conversations with others?

Read the following verses and summarize what they are saying about the power of words:

Not many should become teachers, my brothers, because you know that we will receive a stricter judgment. For we all stumble in many ways. If anyone does not stumble in what he says, he is mature, able also to control the whole body. Now if we put bits into the mouths of horses so that they obey us, we direct their whole bodies. And consider ships: Though very large and driven by fierce winds, they are guided by a very small rudder wherever the will of the pilot directs. So too, though the tongue is a small part of the body, it boasts great things. Consider how a small fire sets ablaze a large forest. And the tongue is a fire. The tongue, a world of unrighteousness, is placed among our members. It stains the whole body, sets the course of life on fire, and is itself set on fire by hell. Every kind of animal, bird, reptile, and fish is tamed and has been tamed by humankind, but no one can tame the tongue. It is a restless evil, full of deadly poison. With the tongue we bless our Lord and Father, and with it we curse people who are made in God's likeness. Blessing and cursing come out of the same mouth. My brothers and sisters, these things should not be this way. Does a spring pour out sweet and bitter water from the same opening? Can a fig tree produce olives, my brothers and sisters, or a grapevine produce figs? Neither can a saltwater spring yield fresh water. –James 3:1-12

Summary:

The tongue of the wise makes knowledge attractive, but the mouth of fools blurts out foolishness. –Proverbs 15:2

Summary:

No foul language should come from your mouth, but only what is good for building up someone in need, so that it gives grace to those who hear. –Ephesians 4:29

Summary:

"Brood of vipers! How can you speak good things when you are evil? For the mouth speaks from the overflow of the heart. A good person produces good things from his storeroom of good, and an evil person produces evil things from his storeroom of evil. I tell you that on the day of judgment people will have to account for every careless word they speak. For by your words you will be acquitted, and by your words you will be condemned." –Matthew 12:34-37

Summary:

If anyone thinks he is religious without controlling his tongue, his religion is useless and he deceives himself. —James 1:26

Summary:

A good person produces good out of the good stored up in his heart. An evil person produces evil out of the evil stored up in his heart, for his mouth speaks from the overflow of the heart. —Luke 6:45

Summary:

Based upon these verses, what is the root cause behind someone who has a speech problem? Why is this important to acknowledge?

The words we say and how we say them mirrors what takes place deep within us. So like other heart issues, honoring God with our words requires our hearts to be transformed by the gospel.

Some people may respond by saying, "I clean up my speech. I can stop cussing and telling bad jokes. I don't need the gospel for that." But you would be just like the Pharisees, saying the right things but still dead inside (Matt. 15:8).

Even if we tried to clean up our own speech, we could only keep up that charade for so long. Eventually we would turn back to our old ways and patterns of speech simply, because lasting transformation can only come from a heart that belongs to Jesus.

The good news is, when Jesus changes our hearts and we receive Him as Lord and King, there is a new ethical impulse within us that drives all of our actions, including our speech towards others.

Read 1 John 4:7-12.

Dear friends, let us love one another, because love is from God, and everyone who loves has been born of God and knows God. The one

who does not love does not know God, because God is love. God's love was revealed among us in this way: God sent his one and only Son into the world so that we might live through him. Love consists in this: not that we loved God, but that he loved us and sent his Son to be the atoning sacrifice for our sins. Dear friends, if God loved us in this way, we also must love one another. No one has ever seen God. If we love one another, God remains in us and his love is made complete in us.
—1 John 4:7-12

What is the ethical impulse that John describes here?

Being the type of people who speak truth in love to those around us requires hearts that need to be motivated out of a genuine love for those people. If we want to be those who don't yell out of anger or make inappropriate jokes and comments, then we have to be motivated out of a love for others. If we want to build up others through the power of encouraging words, then we have to be motivated out of a love for others. Only through love can our words be acceptable and pleasing to God.

PERSONAL STUDY

DAY 1

Isn't it funny how words stick? When I was in elementary school, I talked a lot. In class, I was also very loud. Okay, I talked a lot and I was loud outside of class, too. Pretty much all the time. I still talk a lot and I'm still pretty loud.

In 1980, my 2nd grade teacher gave me a nickname. One day she looked at me and said, "Clayton, you just cannot be quiet. When you talk so loud, you sound so southern and so country. I'm going to start calling you 'The mouth of the south.'"

I still remember what she said, verbatim, because she said it to my face—in front of my entire second grade class. All my friends heard her say it, so of course they called me "mouth of the south" for the rest of that year. The name stuck with me all the way through high school.

Here I am, 35 years later, and I still remember that moment. I remember the words she said. I remember how I felt, and other people remember it, too. Recently I was speaking at a local Christian college and one of my classmates from second grade was there with his son on a campus visit. We hadn't seen each other since high school, and out of the clear blue, he said to me, "Do you remember what your nickname used to be at Shannon Forest?" We both said it in unison, "Mouth of the South!"

What things have people have said to you that you still remember today, even from years ago?

What is one painful memory you have of someone making fun of you or calling you names?

Do you sometimes use your words carelessly? Is this an area of your life that you need to repent of and surrender to Jesus?

Above all, my brothers and sisters, do not swear, either by heaven or by earth or with any other oath. But let your "yes" mean "yes," and your "no" mean "no," so that you won't fall under judgment. –James 5:12

One thing we often do (even when we're unaware) is fail to give a definitive answer with our words. Maybe we're scared of committing to something or afraid of getting locked into a commitment in case something better or more fun comes along. Whether it's making plans and sticking to them or deciding whether or not to be in an exclusive dating relationship, we lean toward being vague and non-committal so we can change plans if we need to or bail out if we don't feel like doing something we don't want to do.

James tells us it's better to simply say no than it is to hover around a decision with indecision. When you say yes to something, follow through with it even if it is hard or inconvenient. If you are not sure about something, then just say no, even if it's only "no" for a season. When you straddle the fence on a decision, it not only affects you, but it also holds other people hostage. It is inconsiderate of their time, energy, and schedule when we go back on our word or back out of a commitment.

This is something that will benefit you as you grow older. Employers, coaches, bosses, friends, and coworkers will all trust you more and enjoy being around you more when they know they can count on you to keep your word once you give it. Don't make excuses. Learn how to look at your schedule and make wise decisions with your "yes" and your "no."

Do you ever feel like you say yes to too many things and then you have to make excuses to back out of things you should have said no to?

Do you ever feel like you make big spiritual commitments (like reading the entire Bible or praying an hour a day) and feel guilty when you fail to complete them? Give a few examples.

There is one who speaks rashly, like a piercing sword; but the tongue of the wise brings healing. –Proverbs 12:18

The week before Sharie and I got married, we attended an event on a local Christian college campus and we had a chance to meet the speaker afterwards. He was a man I had looked up to for a long time and I was excited to get a few minutes with him. Since we were only several days away from our wedding, I asked him for marriage advice.

"We're getting married this Saturday. What kind of great wedding advice can you give us?"

He paused for a long time. He squinted his eyes and pursed his lips. It looked like he was in physical pain as he tried to find the words to answer our question. Then he inhaled, a long, deep breath. He held it, then exhaled and said to me, "You need to say you're sorry." Then he looked at Sharie and said, "When he says he's sorry, you need to forgive him." That was it. He had no more advice. I felt like we got robbed! *Is that all you can say? There has to be more than that, right?*

But over the last two decades, we see now just how wise his advice was. The hardest thing for me (Clayton) to do is to say I am sorry when I mess up. For some reason the words just don't want to form in my mouth. The hardest thing for Sharie to do is to actually forgive me when I finally admit my mistakes.

This verse says the tongue of the wise brings healing, and this is true in every relationship. When you use your words to repent and apologize, it paves the way for healing to begin. When you use your words to extend grace, it finishes the healing work. It makes sense, doesn't it? We cause all kinds of damage and drama with the reckless words we speak. They pierce people like a sword! But we have the same power with our words to heal up the wound our careless words created. Words are both good and bad, used for righteousness and evil. They can wound like a weapon or they can heal like medicine.

Now we have both learned to quickly say we're sorry. This simple biblical wisdom has saved us from so many fights and arguments that would have escalated if we had spoken harshly or recklessly.

Do you tend to defend yourself when you feel like someone expects you to apologize for something?

Do you spend more time explaining yourself to someone you're in conflict with than you do apologizing and listening to them tell you how they feel? If so, why do you think you do this?

What are some practical ways you can use your words to bring healing to others who are close to you?

Can you think of a person you could call, text, or email right now with "healing words" or encouragement or humility of reconciliation?

DAY 4

The one who guards his mouth protects his life; the one who opens his lips invites his own ruin. –Proverbs 13:3

Right after I graduated college, I was over at my pastor's house one night for dinner. We walked down into his basement after desert and he began showing me his personal library. There were over 1,000 books down there, on shelves from wall to way and from floor to ceiling. He told me that he had read almost every one of them and I asked him if he had a life. Turns out he was just really intelligent and way smarter than me.

One book caught my eye; it had a set of lips on the cover. It was called, *Million Dollar Mouths: Seven Secrets of Managers Who Avoid Employee Lawsuits*. I picked it up and flipped through it. It looked sort of boring to be honest, and I put it back on the shelf. My former pastor noticed me holding the book and said, "That's an interesting book right there. It basically takes what the Book of Proverbs says about being wise with your words and keeping your mouth shut, and it applies it to the business world. If people put the wisdom of the Bible into practice they usually don't have to worry about getting sued for libel or slander."

It seems like this book by Stephen D. Bruce tapped into a specific need in the business world back in the mid 1990s. Yet I feel like we need this wisdom in our daily lives now more than ever. This is a strong warning from Scripture. If you never get control of your mouth, and if you move through life speaking harshly about others and to others, you will come to ruin. Did you get that? Your mouth and the words you speak have the ability to ruin your life.

On the flip side, if you guard your lips, you guard your life. This creates an image in my mind. I can see my mouth wanting to say something so bad; a quick comeback, a sarcastic response to someone, a put-down that will put someone in their place. As the words form on my tongue, I remember the wisdom of Proverbs and I close my lips. I press them together. I clinch them tightly and refuse to let the words out. Like guards protecting me from myself, my lips are protecting me from the fallout of the harmful words I almost let fly.

How often to you stop listening to the other person talking because you are planning out in your head what you want to say as soon as they stop?

Do you usually know as soon as you've said something harshly, or do you have to have someone else point it out to you when you do? Explain.

When is the last time you asked the Holy Spirit to help you guard your lips from speaking destructive words?

STUDENTS

Flip to page 112 to continue your study with 30 daily devotions.

LEADERS

Continue to the next page for tips on leading a group through this study.

LEADER GUIDE

SESSION 1: WISDOM

GETTING STARTED

- **Activity (Optional)**. Provide each student with a sheet of paper, instructing them to create a list of requests to God—requests for items, ideas, or skills. After allowing a few minutes, discuss some of their responses, and then refer to the Introduction (p. 4) to see what King Solomon asked for at the beginning of his reign. Afterward, transition to the session overview.

- **Read**. Review the session overview. Begin group time by summarizing the overview for students.

WATCH

Watch the video for Session 1 (included in the DVD Kit). On page 8, students will have space to take notes and fill in answers as they watch.

DISCUSS

Use the group discussion pages to guide your group to respond to the video teaching and relevant Bible passages.

PRAY

As you close group time, ask students for prayer requests. Place students in groups or pairs, depending on the number of students in your group. Invite students to share with their groups situations in which they need wisdom. Then, instruct students to pray for one another in their groups.

WEEKLY LEADER TIPS

- Introduce the personal studies. Tell students you will be completing these studies as well and that they can complete the four studies at their own pace before the group meets again.

- Choose a Scripture that sticks out to you as you walk through the personal studies this week. Text that Scripture to students to encourage them in the middle of the week.

SESSION 2: WISE COUNSEL

GETTING STARTED

- **Review** last week's personal studies with students.

- **Read** the session overview. Begin group time by summarizing the overview for students.

WATCH

Watch the video for Session 2 (included in the DVD Kit). On page 20, students will have space to take notes and fill in answers as they watch.

DISCUSS

Use the group discussion pages to guide your group to respond to the video teaching and relevant Bible passages.

PRAY

As you wrap up today's group session, pray over your students. Ask God to place godly people in their lives who will give them wise counsel. Pray for God to surround them with mentors and friends who will speak truth into their lives and direct them toward God for answers.

WEEKLY LEADER TIPS

- Remind students to complete personal studies.

- Consider finding others who are further along in their faith journey to act as mentors and prayer partners to students. Or assign students accountability partners to encourage and talk with them about the study throughout the week.

SESSION 3: HEART

GETTING STARTED

- **Review** last week's personal studies with students.

- **Read** the session overview. Begin group time by summarizing the overview for students.

WATCH

Watch the video for Session 3 (included in the DVD Kit). On page 32, students will have space to take notes and fill in answers as they watch.

DISCUSS

Use the group discussion pages to guide your group to respond to the video teaching and relevant Bible passages.

PRAY

Invite students to talk about reasons they struggle to fully surrender their hearts to God. Pray that God would reveal those areas to students and how dangerous it is to "listen to your heart." Ask God to help students understand that guarding their hearts doesn't mean being closed off, but rather giving control of their hearts completely to God.

WEEKLY LEADER TIPS

- Ask students about any difficulties with completing last week's personal studies. Encourage them to press through this week's studies and to ask questions when they don't understand.

- Make sure to follow up with students who may have opened up about difficulties with guarding their hearts this week.

SESSION 4: RELATIONSHIPS

- **Review** last week's personal studies with students.

- **Read** the session overview. Begin group time by summarizing the overview for students.

Watch the video for Session 4 (included in the DVD Kit). On page 44, students will have space to take notes and fill in answers as they watch.

Use the group discussion pages to guide your group to respond to the video teaching and relevant Bible passages.

Place students into groups of two or three. Ask students to pray for each of the following: their relationship with God, with believers, and with non-believers. Suggest each student pray choose a topic to pray over. Allow a few minutes, then close by praying for your students to build strong, Christ-centered relationships in all areas of life.

- This week's personal study format is a little different. Be sure to tell students they can continue to complete these as they have time during the week.

- Reach out to students who may have mentioned having broken relationships or difficulties in a particular relationship. Maybe text them a prayer to let them know specifically how you're praying for them.

SESSION 5: ACTIONS AND ATTITUDES

GETTING STARTED

- **Review** last week's personal studies with students.

- **Read** the session overview. Begin group time by summarizing the overview for students.

WATCH

Watch the video for Session 5 (included in the DVD Kit). On page 56, students will have space to take notes and fill in answers as they watch.

DISCUSS

Use the group discussion pages to guide your group to respond to the video teaching and relevant Bible passages.

PRAY

Allow students to go around the room, sharing prayer requests. Tell them to share one request for them and one for someone else. Ask each student to pray for the person to their right. Close by praying for the group.

WEEKLY LEADER TIPS

- Pride isn't something our pride really wants us to address. But, if we don't address the pride in our lives, we will fail to embrace humility. Encourage students to dig deeper into challenging their attitudes and actions through the personal studies this week.

- Challenge students to memorize Proverbs 11:2 and James 4:6, focusing in on what happens to the proud and the humble.

SESSION 6: WORK

GETTING STARTED

- **Review** last week's personal studies with students.

- **Read** the session overview. Begin group time by summarizing the overview for students.

WATCH

Watch the video for Session 6 (included in the DVD Kit). On page 68, students will have space to take notes and fill in answers as they watch.

DISCUSS

Use the group discussion pages to guide your group to respond to the video teaching and relevant Bible passages.

PRAY

Pray over students, asking God to give students the energy, courage, and drive to honor God in all the ways they work.

WEEKLY LEADER TIPS

- Ask students to commit to completing the personal studies this week.

- Send a text or post on social media, reminding students to focus on God as they work—in school, jobs, clubs, chores at home, sports practices, and so on. Consider using Colossians 3:23 as part of your text or post.

SESSION 7: MONEY AND STUFF

- **Review** last week's personal studies with students.

- **Read** the session overview. Begin group time by summarizing the overview for students.

WATCH

Watch the video for Session 7 (included in the DVD Kit). On page 80, students will have space to take notes and fill in answers as they watch.

DISCUSS

Use the group discussion pages to guide your group to respond to the video teaching and relevant Bible passages.

PRAY

Allow students to gather in groups of 2-3 to pray. Suggest students pray for wisdom in the following: managing money and stuff, examining their hearts toward money and stuff, changing opinions about money and stuff to align with God's Word, and how God would have them use the money and stuff they currently have. Close by praying for God to help students set up wise practices now to carry with them into the future.

WEEKLY LEADER TIPS

- Make sure students know they can contact you (and how to do so) if they have questions as they complete the personal studies this week.

- Suggest that students note how much money they spend this week and what they buy or use most often. Making a point to recognize these things can often reveal to us what we treasure most.

SESSION 8: WORDS

GETTING STARTED

- **Review** last week's personal studies with students.

- **Read** the session overview. Begin group time by summarizing the overview for students.

WATCH

Watch the video for Session 8 (included in the DVD Kit). On page 92, students will have space to take notes and fill in answers as they watch.

DISCUSS

Use the group discussion pages to guide your group to respond to the video teaching and relevant Bible passages.

PRAY

Pray over the group, asking God to continue to increase students' wisdom in all areas of their lives. Pray that they will be obedient and seek God first in all they do.

WEEKLY LEADER TIPS

- Remind students to complete personal studies.

- Connect with students who may have mentioned struggling with saying harmful things or being hurt by someone else's words. Commit to listening without judgment and praying with students.

- Since this is the last session, consider gathering one more time to review the last week of personal studies. Meet in a different environment by grabbing lunch or ice cream or even scheduling a fun activity nearby.

30 DAYS

DEVOTIONS

Early in my Christian walk, someone taught me that Solomon asked God for wisdom and God honored his prayer. Wanting to know how to develop my own prayer life, I followed Solomon's lead. I prayed for God to give me wisdom, but after my prayer I didn't feel any smarter than before. Now I know that's because praying for wisdom doesn't work like a magic trick. It just doesn't work like that.

It's no secret that we live in a sinful and confusing world, and while the Holy Spirit guides each Christian in his or her faith, His wisdom doesn't always feel normal or natural to us. In the Old Testament, the Hebrew word for *wise* is used to describe people skillful in working with their hands. In other words, wisdom isn't something theoretical, it's practical and it affects every area of life. Wisdom gives order and purpose to life, discernment in making decisions, and provides a sense of fulfillment in life to the glory of God. Just like we are called to "work out our salvation" (Phil. 2:12), we also have to work to gain wisdom.

Do you want to be the kind of person who applies what you learn? In this devotional, we will study seven ways we can work for the wisdom we seek according to Proverbs 22:1-5. We'll learn how to be grounded in:

1. wisdom by accepting God's words.

2. righteousness by storing His commands within us.

3. our actions and attitudes by listening closely to wisdom.

4. our hearts by learning to direct them to understanding.

5. our wise counsel by asking for insight and understanding.

6. our treasure by seeking wisdom as if it is silver.

7. our work by applying God's knowledge.

Pray for God to help you become grounded in the wisdom He offers. We believe the pages that follow will help you receive the wisdom He has promised you.

When I speak, people often ask, "In your message, you said you heard God speak to you. I've never heard God. How does God speak to you, and how do you hear Him?" Many people think God hasn't spoken to them because they haven't heard an audible voice from heaven. But let me tell you a little secret: God very rarely speaks audibly. Most of the time, we hear His voice through His Word, the leading of the Holy Spirit, or through other believers as they challenge and encourage us. So, if we want to hear God's voice, we have to make time to read His Word, to pray and listen to the Holy Spirit, and to accept advice from our friends and those in authority over us.

Most of us know we need to read the Bible more and listen to wise people, so I believe our biggest hang up is listening to the guidance of the Holy Spirit. You may feel as if you've never heard God's voice, but Proverbs 8:35-36 says otherwise:

> *For the one who finds me finds life and obtains favor from the LORD, but the one who misses me harms himself; all who hate me love death."*
> —Proverbs 8:35-36

Every person who has given their life to Jesus has heard and responded to the voice of the Holy Spirit. We cannot become believers unless God reveals to us that we are sinners who need Jesus to save us. Therefore, if you heard and responded to Jesus' call to salvation, you have heard the voice of God. Your willingness to believe the message of salvation is proof that you can hear the voice of God!

You may not think you are wise compared to your teachers, your pastor, or your parents, but if you have responded to Jesus then you are wiser than those in our world who refuse to believe the gospel. Jesus' message often seems ridiculous to our world, but the fact that you listened proves you love God's wisdom more than the world's foolish doctrine. Your salvation was the wisest choice you could've ever made, but there's so much more wisdom for you to gain.

Have you ever experienced spiritual doubt? Have you ever been confident in your faith one minute only to fall into confusion the next? Perhaps a tough life circumstance, the consequences of a bad decision, or someone else's strong opinion shifted your thinking from faith to doubt. When sin came into the world, it brought all sorts of destructive doctrines. We have to fight and filter these doubts, thoughts, and ideas from our minds. If you've experienced doubt, please know you're not the only one. But with this consolation, I also offer this assurance from Proverbs 1:20-23:

> *Wisdom calls out in the street; she makes her voice heard in the public squares. She cries out above the commotion; she speaks at the entrance of the city gates: "How long, inexperienced ones, will you love ignorance? How long will you mockers enjoy mocking and you fools hate knowledge? If you respond to my warning, then I will pour out my spirit on you and teach you my words.* –Proverbs 1:20-23

Even you will sometimes experience doubt and confusion in life, you don't have to remain oppressed by it because wisdom is always available to you. This passage says wisdom calls out and makes herself heard, even above the chaos. So, when doubt and confusion arise, wisdom is not quiet! You might have to change the channel you're listening to, but these verses leave no doubt that wisdom is accessible, loud and obvious if you listen closely.

You will have to train your ears to hear. You will have to leave behind the ignorant theories you're used to and listen closely to hear God's warning. When you do, God will honor you and give you everything you need to live a godly life.

DAY 4

TRUSTING WISDOM

James, the brother of Jesus, said God will generously give us wisdom when we ask.

> *Now if any of you lacks wisdom, he should ask God—who gives to all generously and ungrudgingly—and it will be given to him. But let him ask in faith without doubting. For the doubter is like the surging sea, driven and tossed by the wind. That person should not expect to receive anything from the Lord, being double-minded and unstable in all his ways.* —James 1:5-8

These verses tell me a few things:

- If I need wisdom I should ask God.

- God generously gives wisdom without judgment.

- When He speaks, I need to believe what He says.

- When He speaks, if I doubt, I will become confused and not believe He spoke to me.

- When He speaks, I will receive His wisdom if I believe He spoke to me. If I doubt, my confusion will keep me from receiving it.

Read James 1:22-25.

Summarize the truth of this passage in your own words.

If you're going to ask God to help you, believe He will. Believe He will speak, and then make yourself quiet and wait for the answer. Don't ask and ignore. Trust His advice. Ask, listen, and do what He says. If God promises to speak to you and you aren't hearing, perhaps you're either not listening, or you just need a little more practice. Don't ever give up!

Recently I took a spiritual gifts test and according to the results, my primary gifts are discernment, knowledge, and teaching. When I saw my results, I was filled with mixed emotions because the results felt true to me, but my first thought was, "Who wants to hang out with the spiritual nerd?" When I was in high school, I was free spirited and fun with my friends, but I became guarded in situations where I felt pressure to compromise my faith. I loved friends and fun, but I also wanted to be wise. Sometimes, making the wise choice felt more like a punishment than a reward. I often regretted saying no to temptation, because my choice left me feeling lonely and left out. Wisdom doesn't always feel rewarding. In fact, to our flesh, it can feel downright disappointing.

Friend, if you're feeling this way, please hear me: Wise decisions are worth it. Don't give in. When your friends think you are crazy for saying no, remember that wisdom will produce greater results in your life than your friends' approval. Don't let your lonely feelings deceive you. Wisdom is the better choice.

Read Proverbs 2:6-15.

What stands out to you in this passage?

When we make the wise choice, the Lord will give you success and be your shield. He will guard your path and protect your way. Your friends may consider your wise choices old fashioned and ridiculous, but when your life is blessed and the path is straight, you will be proud of listening to Jesus. God's wisdom promises to rescue us from evil and from anyone who means to harm us. Cherishing God's wisdom is always the best thing you can do, even if it doesn't feel that way in the moment.

How do you plan to apply these truths to your life this week?

DAY 6

GROUNDED IN RIGHTEOUSNESS

In the beginning, God made Adam and Eve in His own image. They were full of goodness and devoid of all evil. But one day, a serpent who hated God visited Adam and Eve in the garden. Because he hated God, he also hated Adam and Eve—they were good, reflecting God's own goodness. The serpent wanted to put a wedge between God and His creation, so he caused them to doubt God's goodness toward them. He convinced the man and woman that God's rules were keeping them from something good instead of protecting them from something evil. The serpent said, "God knows that when you eat it your eyes will be opened and you will be like God, knowing good and evil" (Gen. 3:5). This part of the serpent's statement was true. The man and woman already knew good, but when they ate the fruit, they also became aware of evil. But God didn't want Adam and Eve to eat the fruit because He didn't want them to have to experience evil. In fact, His rule was meant to protect them from the consequences of evil.

Write out your personal definition of sin.

Now, let me define sin for you. Sin is evil; it is disobedience. Sin became a part of the human race when Adam and Eve chose to trust their own reasoning over their Creator's guidance. As the mother and father of the human race, Adam and Eve have handed this sin down to each one of us. Therefore, sin lives in each of us. While Jesus' death on the cross saves us from the eternal punishment of our sins, we will still struggle with sin while we live on this earth. But, here is the greatest news of all: James says, "Blessed is the one who endures trials, because when he has stood the test he will receive the crown of life that God has promised to those who love him" (1:12).

The devil knows just what to say to persuade and turn us against our Lord. If we don't want to be easily lured into his trap, we have to direct our hearts to surrender to our Creator's wisdom instead of our own.

The Huffington Post has an article called, "10 Most Notorious Criminals in American History." If you read the list of these criminal offenses, they include things like: distribution of illegal alcohol and drugs, murder, gambling, prostitution, race wars, domestic terrorism, professional killing, bombings, kidnapping, and cultist activities.[1] When I read about such egregious crimes, I can't help but wonder how a person comes to a mental, emotional, and spiritual condition to commit these felonies. It seems unbelievable that someone's heart can become so hard that it no longer feels guilt and stops responding to conviction.

People don't usually transition from exemplary citizen to hardened criminal overnight. Thieves aren't born to rob banks. They start slowly by lying, deceiving, and feeding their greed. Sin is progressive. At first unwise choices seem inconsequential, but they eventually morph into destructive habits that numb our souls to wisdom. James explains how sin works like this: "Then after desire has conceived, it gives birth to sin, and when sin is fully grown, it gives birth to death" (1:15). Our desires, when fed and nurtured in our hearts and minds, inevitably lead to action. When those desires are ungodly, so too is the resulting behavior.

How have you seen sin start small and grow into habits in your own life?

Just like Adam and Eve, we are all susceptible to sin, but the way we handle it determines how sin will handle us. When we give in and act on our evil desires, sin is born. If we continue in our sin, instead of repenting, it will bring us death.

> *Whoever lives with integrity fears the LORD, but the one who is devious in his ways despises him.* –Proverbs 14:2

The Word of God says sin brings death to your life. To live a life of integrity and fear of the Lord means we have a healthy fear of the affect of sin on our lives. How will you choose to handle your sin? Will you welcome or resist sin? Wisdom calls you to resist (Jas. 4:7).

DAY 8
UNDERSTANDING THE LAW

When my bike still had training wheels, I tried to imagine what it would be like to ride unencumbered. I played out the scenario in my mind. Mom and I walking up to the top of our cul-de-sac, mounting my bike, and my mom giving me a little boost down the hill. I could see me riding with my arms held wide. But, then the day came. Fear entered my blood as my mom removed my training wheels; my safety net was gone. I was so afraid. What if I failed? What if I fell?

We walked to the top of the hill. I mounted my bike, and mom gave me a little push. For a minute it worked until my front wheel started wobbling and I overcompensated. The entire situation ended with me screaming, two very skinned knees, and no desire to ever ride a bike again. The training wheels had protected me, but once I decided to go at it on my own, I fell.

When have you been afraid of falling?

Similarly, the law protects us from sin. If we love and trust God's instruction, obeying it will bring us peace. But if you fight against it, your sin nature will convince you that you don't need God's protection. Here are two ways the law protects you:

1. FIRST. GOD USES THE LAW TO REVEAL YOUR SIN AND NEED FOR SALVATION. Think about it. If the law didn't exist, you wouldn't know wrong from right. God used the law to lead you into a relationship with Jesus and to give you eternal life.

2. THE LAW SERVES AS A GUIDELINE TO KEEP US FROM FALLING INTO SINFUL PATTERNS. When we break the law, the Lord uses discipline to bring us back to righteousness. No discipline seems enjoyable at the time, but painful. Later on, however, it yields the peaceful fruit of righteousness to those who have been trained by it.

When did you first recognize your sin and need for salvation? What role did the law play in that realization?

UNDERSTANDING CONSEQUENCES

When I was little my mom let us watch *Looney Tunes*. Ironically, I didn't like this cartoon; it tore me up emotionally. I felt sorry for Wiley Coyote. First of all, he never caught the Road Runner, and secondly his life always ended with a splat. Then, there was poor Donald Duck. The poor guy was always trying to decide whether to listen to the devil on one shoulder or the angel on the other. Multiple episodes were dedicated to this foolish duck's propensity to make the wrong choice. As if making the wrong choice wasn't excruciating enough, his inability to come clean and confess his misdeeds usually created more drama.

Donald was always making mistakes, but he never learned from them. He is the ultimate definition of a fool. In the last devotion, we talked about how God's law is a gift. Well, consequences are gifts, too. Proverbs 1:29-33 explains how when we choose to sin, God uses the consequences of our sin to teach us.

> *"Because they hated knowledge, didn't choose to fear the LORD, were not interested in my counsel, and rejected all my correction, they will eat the fruit of their way and be glutted with their own schemes. For the apostasy of the inexperienced will kill them, and the complacency of fools will destroy them. But whoever listens to me will live securely and be undisturbed by the dread of danger."* –Proverbs 1:29-33

God does not force us to obey him. Instead, He allows us to suffer the consequences of our own choices. He will use the misery sin brings into our lives to show us His plan is better and turn our hearts back to him. When we make sinning a habit, we become like fools. But, if we listen to God's counsel and receive His correction, we will live securely. The choice to sin or to obey is yours.

When have you chosen to disobey God? What happened?

DAY 10

My (Sharie) last two years of high school were full of transition. A wave of students and teachers left my junior year, which brought in a new tide of students and teachers. The change disturbed my security like a riptide pulling me into deep waters. Many of my good friends left, and the new ones became increasingly interested in partying and recreational relationships. I resisted for a bit, but I grew tired of being lonely so accepted invitations to two parties and started dating a guy who I knew was wrong for me. I hadn't tuned out wisdom, in fact I heard her warning me about my bad decisions, but I *chose* not to listen. After a few instances of mild rebellious dabbling, I just couldn't continue to disobey. I repented before my decisions produced devastating consequences, but I lived with a lot of guilt for making bad decisions when I "should have known better."

When have you given in to temptation? Explain.

What is temptation? Temptation is anything that attracts us or draws our attention and desire; it is seductive. James said "each person is tempted when he is drawn away and enticed by his own evil desire" (1:14). So, temptation is a desire that tries to seduce us into sin and away from obedience to our Savior. However, when we are tempted, we do not have to sin if we are truly found in Christ and have His Spirit living within us. When Jesus lived on earth, He was tempted in every way, but never sinned. Because He was tempted, we have a High Priest and Savior who knows our struggles and weaknesses, offering grace and help when we need it (Heb. 4:15-16).

When have you been tempted and clearly seen the way of escape God provided (1 Cor. 10:13)?

When I became a Christian, I thought right choices would come naturally and temptation would subside as I became a better and better Christian. I thought being a Christian would remove my desire to sin. Honestly, I thought God would make me choose righteousness, but right choices didn't come naturally. I still wanted to sin and God didn't "make me" do the right thing. Just as God doesn't tempt us, neither does He force us into obedience. He is more interested in us becoming like Him than controlling our behavior.

So, if we are prone to sin and God isn't going to make us choose righteousness, how are we supposed to overcome temptation? I want to provide you with three action steps to help you overcome temptation. They are: Resist, Remember, and Repent.

1. RESIST. Since the desire to sin doesn't disappear when we become Christians, we have to create new thought patterns and habits to teach us to become slaves to righteousness instead of slaves to sin (Rom. 6:15-23). James advises, "submit to God. Resist the devil, and he will flee from you. Draw near to God, and he will draw near to you" (4:7-8).

2. REMEMBER. When temptation comes your way, one way to overcome and resist it is to remember the misery of feeling distant from God. Also, remind yourself of how much you hate sin's consequences. I'm not suggesting you wallow in misery and shame, but to use these feelings as a catalyst to resist the devil and draw near to God.

3. REPENT. When I sin, I usually want to copy Adam and Eve or try to cover my sin with good deeds. Neither of these actions alleviate my guilt or restore my relationship with God. The only way to overcome temptation when you've given in is to humble yourself and repent to God. James said, "Cleanse your hands, sinners, and purify your hearts, you double-minded. Be miserable and mourn and weep. Let your laughter be turned to mourning and your joy to gloom. Humble yourselves before the Lord, and he will exalt you" (4:8-10).

DAY 12

ACTIONS AND ATTITUDES

Did you know that a significant portion of Americans spend more than eight hours a day on their devices or using social media . More than any time period before, we have more leisure but we are choosing entertainment over education. What does any of this have to do with God or our relationship with Jesus? Take a minute to read Psalm 1:1-6:

> *How happy is the one who does not walk in the advice of the wicked*
> *or stand in the pathway with sinners or sit in the company of mockers!*
> *Instead, his delight is in the LORD's instruction, and he meditates on*
> *it day and night. He is like a tree planted beside flowing streams that*
> *bears its fruit in its season and whose leaf does not wither. Whatever he*
> *does prospers. The wicked are not like this; instead, they are like chaff*
> *that the wind blows away. Therefore the wicked will not stand up in the*
> *judgment, nor sinners in the assembly of the righteous. For the LORD*
> *watches over the way of the righteous, but the way of the wicked leads*
> *to ruin.* –Psalm 1:1-6

These verses very clearly state that the one who listens, delights and meditates on God's Word will be happy. In other words, when our actions are grounded in God's Word, we will be like trees planted right beside water, always having access to God's presence, wisdom, and joy. This sounds dreamy, but there is a catch. We cannot store up, delight in, or obey God's commands if we don't focus our attention on reading, studying, and listening.

Are you grounded in your actions and attitudes? Are you using your time and technology to bring you closer to God? If not, decide to use your phone instead of letting your phone use you. Set a specific reminder to pray, study, and journal so you don't get distracted. Challenge your friends to study with you during lunch, or before or after school.

Here's the bottom line. Being grounded in your actions and attitudes requires time and effort. How you decide to invest your time directly affects your happiness. Where will you invest?

When I first became a Christian I often felt heavy in my heart when I was around friends who didn't know Jesus. I felt inexplicably sad and deflated. I didn't understand why I felt this way and often felt like I was the party pooper. Have you ever felt troubled around your lost friends or your Christian friends who aren't taking Jesus seriously? If so, I want to encourage you. This is a godly emotion, which is often described as a burden. A burden is a feeling or desire you carry for someone else. You might feel burdened if someone you love doesn't know Jesus, is making an unwise decision, or has lost their passion for the Lord.

You may be wondering, "If this is a godly emotion, why does it feel so bad?" Well, just before Jesus' death—when He was praying in the Garden of Gethsemane—He was burdened, too. Jesus took His disciples to a quiet place to pray, and even though they feel asleep, Jesus continued to pray through the night. His body was filled with such deep emotion that His blood vessels burst and blood escaped through the capillaries in His skin (Luke 22:24). This burden doesn't sound pleasant, but aren't we all thankful for Jesus' faithfulness to carry this burden for us? He did not give up, and we are able to reap the benefit of the emotional heaviness He felt in that moment.

When you want your friends to know Jesus and reap the benefits of a godly life, you are carrying a burden just like Him.

> If you do nothing in a difficult time, your strength is limited. Rescue those being taken off to death, and save those stumbling toward slaughter. If you say, "But we didn't know about this," won't he who weighs hearts consider it? Won't he who protects your life know? Won't he repay a person according to his work? —Proverbs 24:10-12

When we became Christians, we also became ambassadors, or representatives, of God in this world. We are His voice, His hands and His feet. We are called to show sinners why life with Christ is better.

When have you been able to show/tell someone that life with Christ is better? Explain.

DAY 14
LOVING THE LOST (PART 2)

When I was in college, I learned it's not my job to save people. Even as I type these words to you, this confession sounds weird because we know Jesus is the only One who can save us. Still, somehow I adopted the belief that God expected me to save people from their sin. My eyes were opened as I read the parable of the growing seed (Mark 4:26-29). I noticed the farmer, who represented me, was responsible for spreading the seeds on the ground while the Lord watered them and caused them to grow.

We should feel burdened for our friends who don't yet know Jesus and are struggling with their sin, but we must carry this burden well. We are responsible for scattering seeds, using our lives as opportunities to show people what loving Jesus looks like. But we are not responsible for making people grow or forcing their decision to follow Christ.

Sharing Jesus with our friends can be intimidating so I want to give you three key attitudes to help relieve any fear. These come from James 3:13-18.

1. SEEK TO UNDERSTAND INSTEAD OF BEING UNDERSTOOD.
   If you are wise, your words should be laced with gentleness and understanding. If you want your friends to listen, you need to have an attitude of understanding. Too often I've seen Christians speak about sin with an attitude of condemnation rather than mercy and guidance.

2. SPEAK THE TRUTH IN LOVE. Some of us are good at speaking a lot of truth with little love, while others of us are good at speaking a lot of love with little truth. Ephesians 4:15 says we need to speak the "truth in love." Truth without love is harsh and love without truth lacks grit.

3. EMBRACE HUMILITY INSTEAD OF JUDGMENT. When our friends' lives are falling apart it's easy to become motivated by fear and sit in judgment instead of adopting a posture of humility and trust in God. You may have the "perfect" solution to their dilemma, but they may not be in a place to receive it. It's more important to be real than right. Your friend will be more motivated to change through love than from a lecture.

When you think about loving someone through your actions, what comes to mind? Perhaps buying someone a meal, giving them your favorite shirt, or maybe offering them a ride? These are certainly good deeds. But I want to challenge you for a minute. Can you remember a time you felt absolutely desperate for help? Maybe one of your friends gossiped about you, telling your friends something you wanted kept secret. Or perhaps you felt pressured to make a decision you now regret and you feel like there's no going back. Here's my point. It's always good to give someone food, clothing or assistance, but how much more should we offer our friends spiritual or emotional courage?

Here are some practical ways to support your friends.

1. WATCH OUT FOR FOOLS. Stay away from foolish people. Keep your emotions and feelings on guard against anyone who is trying to make it easy for you or your friends to disobey Jesus. Anyone who encourages you to participate in "reckless living" is not acting like a friend.

2. USE YOUR EARS. Take time to listen to God (Prov. 8:34-36). We cannot be filled with the Spirit if we don't spend time with him.

3. USE YOUR WORDS. You are called to be your friends' best cheerleader, encouraging them to live wisely and in step with the Spirit. Ephesians says we should be praising and thanking God together (5:19-21). Listen to and sing praise music with one another. Learn Scripture and use it in your daily life. Encourage your friends with Scripture and submit yourself to them if they correct you with it. Use your words to strengthen your friends instead of tearing them down.

When have you been able to use your words for someone else's good? What happened? How can you practice this throughout the week?

DAY 16

GROUNDED IN MY HEART

I almost started this devotion off with this statement, "When I was a teenager, one of my biggest fears was rejection and loneliness," but here's the reality; adults are afraid of being disliked and alone as well. So,let me start by saying, "Some of my biggest fears are rejection and loneliness." In fact, I made most of my mistakes because I was afraid. Fear of failing. Fear of surviving. Fear of trying to please someone. We can become afraid of just about anything.

We date the wrong person because we're afraid to be alone. We might to choose unhealthy forms of entertainment, like parties or porn, because we don't want to be isolated from the group. Perhaps we disrespect our parents and teachers because we're more concerned with pleasing our friends than honoring our authorities.

Who are you most afraid of disappointing?

If you let Jesus show you the motivation of your heart, you might discover many of your choices originate in fear; specifically fear of people. Well, God did not design you to be a people pleaser, but to be a God pleaser.

Do you want to please God? Do you want him to remove your fear of people? If so, you must learn how to properly fear the Lord.

> *The fear of the LORD is the beginning of knowledge; fools despise wisdom and discipline.* –Proverbs 1:7

> *The fear of the LORD is the beginning of wisdom; all who follow his instructions have good insight. His praise endures forever.*
> –Psalm 111:10

Wisdom is about fearing the right thing, or rather, the right person. When you fear God you don't have to fear anything else.

When I was in elementary school, I (Sharie) crushed on a boy for a long time before he asked if I'd be his girlfriend. It feels silly to admit that I said yes to being his girlfriend. I didn't even know what I was agreeing to, but it didn't matter anyway because he broke my heart before I could find out. He "broke up" with me the next day because he was more interested in a girl who was able to pull out chunks of her hair. (I guess that was attractive in elementary school.) I was mad. I even considered pulling clumps of my hair out as well to prove my love and devotion, but changed my mind once I really considered the consequences.

What kind of guy likes a girl because she pulls out her hair? This seems ridiculous, but you have to admit our hearts experience a lot of unreasonable and tricky emotions. As the prophet Jeremiah said,

> The heart is more deceitful than anything else, and incurable—who can understand it? I, the Lord, examine the mind, I test the heart to give to each according to his way, according to what his actions deserve.
> —Jeremiah 17:9-10

Our hearts may be confusing and deceitful, but God knows how to understand our minds and hearts. If we are repentant and willing to follow God's Word, the Holy Spirit will show us when our hearts are drifting away from the truth and will guide us back onto the right path. The Word should be bound to the heart (Ps. 119:11), because the heart is the "source of life" (Prov. 4:23). If we want to direct our hearts well, we must be grounded in wisdom and guard them.

For every evil temptation your heart wants pursue exists a better direction of pursuit. When you want to gossip, find something encouraging to say instead. When you feel jealousy rising up, search for something that makes you thankful. Our heart is our source of life, so whatever we love will leak out. If we want to leak wisdom instead of foolishness, we have to stay on God's path and keep our feet from evil.

What will you do to direct your heart toward God this week?

DAY 18

GROUNDED IN WHO I LOVE

"Falling in love" is a glamorized American idea that has taken root in so many minds and hearts as the point of life. Many believe if you could just fall in love with the right person, your life would be complete. But I know, as a father and a husband, that adults are just as fickle as teenagers when it comes to falling in and out of love. In the past five years, I have watched 12 close friends fall out of love with their spouses and fall in love with someone they were not married to, divorce their spouses in order to turn the sinful affair into a new marriage, and leave their wife or husband behind for a "new love."

Proverbs 10:9 says, "The one who lives with integrity lives securely, but whoever perverts his ways will be found out." In other words, you walk securely when you take a straight path in life, but when you take a crooked path, you will suffer and you will be found out. Take a straight path in deciding now the kind of person you will love. You can be grounded in your heart when you choose, as a young man or woman, to only pursue love with a person who embodies godly character and integrity. But this will not happen accidentally. You will need to aggressively pursue this if you want to one day enter a marriage covenant that will stand the test of time and the testing of this fallen and broken world.

- Choose to love someone who is humble enough to listen and admit they're wrong (Prov. 10:8).

- Choose to love someone who isn't lazy but is willing to work (Prov. 10:4).

- Choose to love someone who is wise enough to keep their mouth shut (Prov. 10:19).

- Choose to love someone who uses their words to build up instead of tearing others down or spreading negativity (Prov. 10:31).

   Now, ask yourself: Do these qualities describe me? If so, ask God to strengthen those qualities in you. If not, ask God to show you how to become a wise person.

When I was a teenager love looked like an incurable disease. Students jumped in and out of relationships, elated one minute and depressed the next. School no longer felt like a place for learning, but a fish bowl of hormone motivated teenagers throwing theology and God to the wind while feeding themselves on the world's idea of sexuality. But love is not irresistible and irrational, elating you one minute and throwing you in to confusion the next. Love is patient and kind, not rude or self-seeking (1 Cor. 13). But when we throw wisdom to the wind, the way we love becomes distorted, damaging our hearts and the person we are trying to love.

Read Psalm 26:2-3.

God's faithful love is supposed to guide us as we live by his truth. If you are chasing love, but you are running from Jesus' truth and the wisdom of others, you are pursing a foolish form of love.

In Proverbs 7, Solomon tells us about a young, inexperienced man. He is walking along the street one night when he comes upon a prostitute with a "hidden agenda."

> *She seduces him with her persistent pleading; she lures with her flattering talk. He follows her impulsively like an ox going to the slaughter, like a deer bounding toward a trap until an arrow pierces its liver, like a bird darting into a snare—he doesn't know it will cost him his life.* —Proverbs 7:21-23

By going to her house, her table, and her bed, the young man willfully disobeyed God. If he had looked up to the Lord and remembered His Word (v. 24), looked within and kept his heart focused on God's truth (v. 25), and looked ahead to see the terrible consequences of his sin (vv. 26-27), he would have turned around and fled from the temptation. If we want to be properly grounded in love, we must let truth dictate how we love instead of giving into unbridled passion.

DAY 20

GROUNDED IN HOW I HEAL

No matter how slowly you enter into relationships, how much wisdom you exercise in friendships, or how committed you are to purity before marriage, this simple fact is inevitable: You will get hurt. Then you will have to heal.

That is how life works. To love is to open yourself up to pain and disappointment. To truly love, you have to be vulnerable. When we are vulnerable, we allow ourselves to get close enough to another person where they can return that love back to us. In that place, they can also deeply wound us by letting us down, failing us, breaking a promise to us, or betraying our trust. That sounds like bad news, I know. But the good news is simply this: God can heal you when you get hurt.

When have you been hurt by someone you loved?

There is one who speaks rashly, like a piercing sword; but the tongue of the wise brings healing. –Proverbs 12:18

To be grounded in your healing means being close to the true source of healing—those who speak wisdom.

Who has God used to speak wisdom or bring healing into your life?

God heals us when we are hurt by those we love, and He does it both through His Word and brothers and sisters in Christ who use their words to bring encouragement, kindness, and comfort. This has happened to me countless times.

Be grounded in your healing. Don't numb yourself with pills, alcohol, social media, Netflix, or ice cream. Don't turn to the world's music or entertainment or resort to self-harm. You will never heal by getting into a "revenge relationship" to try to hurt the person who hurt you. Let God heal you, and let Him use the church to be that source of healing for you when relationships break your heart.

A few months ago, I (Sharie) decided to drive downtown and write in one of my favorite coffee shops. It was such a perfect day that I couldn't find a parking spot on the street, so I opted for the parking garage. I have an SUV, so I decided to park in an open area of the garage. But when I left five hours later, I found my car sandwiched by three other SUV's. I started to panic.

In case you haven't ever been in this situation, let me explain. Even if your SUV is modestly sized, when three oversized SUV's are parked behind you in a parking garage it's almost impossible to get out. Here's what it looked like: Back up. Pull forward. Stop. Get out to determine how much room I still have to maneuver. Get back in. Repeat. Give up. Cry. Call my husband to tell him I am trapped in a parking garage forty minutes away. Pull myself together and try it all again.

I kept trying until I clearly avoid every obstacle. As I drove home processing my anger at the parking garage designers, I realized it would have been so much easier if someone had been with me. I just needed one person to guide me, keep me safe and give me a better perspective of my situation.

When have you experienced something similar?

Now, make a list of the steps you have taken to solve your problem.

Have you asked someone wiser than you for advice, or have you spent most of your energies complaining to your friends? Are you satisfied talking in circles about your issue, or do you want a solution to your problem? Drama may be addicting and entertaining, but it isn't life giving. If you want to live wisely, you must give thought to your steps, find the straight path, and ask for advice. What action step will you make today?

I (Sharie) once had a conversation with a young girl who was living with a family. She expressed her concern over their parenting style and was concerned their kids would turn out spoiled. As I listened, I felt compassion for the couple. When I was her age, I had so many ideas of how I would parent, the things I would and wouldn't do. But, when I was twenty-six, the doctor placed my first child in my arms, and I thought, "Oh Jesus, I don't have any clue how to raise this little boy!" I had imagined being a mom. I had imagined succeeding as a mom, but the reality of motherhood put the fear of God in me.

I know you're not a mom or a dad yet, but you have one. Have you ever put yourself in their shoes? Have you wondered how intimidating it feels to be a parent; or what it's like to raise you? After my children were born, I was scared to discipline them too much or not enough. I was scared to love them too much or not enough. I was scared of being overprotective or giving them too much independence. There are a million parenting books, but none of them were written specifically about you. Although your parents probably wish they had all the answers, they don't.

Look, parenting isn't easy so your parents will inevitably mess up. You will probably catch them in all kinds of inconsistencies. Maybe you will see their sin flare up every now and then. When this happens, remind yourself that they are just people, too. However imperfect they are, if you are willing to submit yourself to them, the Lord will see your heart and honor your attitude.

When is it difficult to obey your parents? How does it help you to know God sees your heart and will honor you when it's in the right place?

It's easy to judge what you haven't experienced. If you continue to judge and criticize your parents, you will stunt your spiritual growth and may one day feel your judgmental finger pointing back at you. But if you approach your parents with an attitude of obedience you will become mature and knowledgeable.

Clayton and I had just finished leading a trip in Israel and crossed the border into Jordan. We wanted to explore the places Moses and the Israelites traveled after their exodus from Egypt. Our guide led us through a barren desert to the top of Mount Nebo, the traditional burial site of Moses.

Our guide was telling us about the church on the top of Mount Nebo when he paused and pointed to a line of shrubs. He turned to us and asked, "Do you know the name of this shrub?" We all shrugged our shoulders no, so he answered, "This is the Desert Oleander. Although it is very beautiful, it is also very poisonous. If you ever want to know if a plant is safe, watch how the animals interact with it and you will know which plants to avoid."

The oleander shrub on top of the desert area of Mount Nebo had bright green leaves with luscious red flowers. To the senses it appeared beneficial, but the birds knew it was full of poison so they would not go near it. To the eyes, there seemed to be no sustenance surrounding this shrub, but as we drove away from the mountain I noticed hundreds of sheep and birds living off the less enchanting shrubs on the mountain's slopes. To my eyes, the bright green leaves and red flowers seemed better than the lonely, beige plants, but the wildlife knew better.

What are some things in your life that look beautiful on the outside, but have harmed you or have the potential to harm you? Explain.

Like the desert oleander, sin will tempt you. So if you want to be grounded in wisdom, you must seek out wise counsel. Just like our guide advised us to learn from nature, you must choose to learn from wiser Christians who have more experience. Sometimes righteous choices feel barren and lonely, but if you choose wisdom, God promises you will flourish. God's mission is, and will always be, to protect and provide for you.

List the names of a few wiser Christians you know. How can you learn from them?

DAY 24
GROUNDED IN SPIRITUAL HEALTH

If you were to picture someone who is spiritually healthy, who would you imagine? Perhaps a pastor, a speaker, or a worship leader? What makes them seem spiritually healthy to you? The lyrics to their music or expression when they sing? Their passion or ability to talk about the Bible so beautifully? Perhaps it's just the way they carry themselves or the image they project?

How do you define spiritual health? How does God define it?

I have specifically chosen four verses to show you how to guard your soul and ground yourself spiritually. Let's walk through them together.

1. GIVE GOD COMPLETE ACCESS TO YOUR HEART. Sin wants to trick us into thinking we are living a pure life while our insides rot away, so we have to give God complete access to weigh our motives and to discipline us (Prov. 16:2).

2. PROTECT YOURSELF FROM FALSE TEACHING. In Titus 1:15-16, Paul rebuked leaders who had an appearance of godliness, but who preached a false gospel. He said these leaders could no longer distinguish pure from impure.

3. STAY HUMBLE AND LISTEN TO AUTHORITY. The Lord and those in authority over you are your best protection against sin, so don't absorb the lie that Christianity and the Bible are old fashioned. Don't believe the lie that you know everything you need to know (Prov. 30:11-13).

4. FOCUS ON YOUR INSIDE CONDITION. In Matthew 23:25-26, Jesus was frustrated with the religious leaders because they were more focused on looking religious than the condition of their souls. Legalism is one of the biggest blinders to being spiritually healthy because doing good feels good. But who we are becoming is more important than what we are doing. Our salvation and who we become isn't even about doing better; it's about letting Jesus transform you into someone new.

Years ago, someone stole from Clayton and I. It was an open and shut case where we could have taken the guy to court and won, but we were compelled by the Lord and our elders at our church to give this person a chance to repent and reconcile. He did not. Years later, we shared this story with someone we were discipling and he flat out asked, "Why didn't you take that guy for all he was worth?" It had been years since the fiasco. My husband and I looked at each other and responded in unison, "It wouldn't have been worth it."

This may sound super spiritual to you, but I say this in deep humility: We decided to trust the Lord to carry us through what seemed like an impossible situation, and He did.

Let me explain. Not long after this situation, Clayton was preaching at an event where a couple overheard Clayton talking about a discipleship program our ministry was about to launch. We needed money to purchase a building for the program and were low on funds. The week after Clayton returned home, a check arrived in the mail to cover the entire amount.

I'm not going to lie. During that crisis, we often wanted to take things into our own hands. We wanted justice, but we denied ourselves and continually submitted ourselves to Jesus, not knowing what the future held. But when we held that check in our hands, we knew the Lord had seen our pain and chose to meet our needs. We watched Proverbs 3:34 come true right in front of our eyes, "He mocks those who mock, but gives grace to the humble."

When you're having trouble submitting yourself to God's wisdom and sovereignty, remember these three principles:

1. God gives favor to the humble.

2. He resists the proud, but gives grace to the humble.

3. He lifts up those who humble themselves.

DAY 26
GROUNDED IN MY TREASURE

When your newest, latest, or greatest obsession is available, what do you do? One of my sons used to have an obsession with shoes. A couple of years ago, we were traveling in the car when a new shoe was released. The minute they released, he frantically tried to order them from every website and app available to him on his phone, but his phone started timing out. So, he tried our phones, which also timed out. Trying to assuage his anxiety, we stopped at Starbucks so he could use the internet. When that didn't work, he started calling relatives who lived near shoe stores to find out if they would pick him up a pair.

Just like my son let himself become worked up when he couldn't get his hands on those shoes, I can also let the wrong things become my treasure. People often tell me that they don't read their Bibles, and when I ask why, they say they don't have time.

Honestly, this is my go to excuse for not making space for God, but do you really think this is a reasonable excuse? Do we really not have time for God, or are we simply choosing to use our time for other things (movies, sports, hanging out with friends, binging on entertainment, school, youth group, texting, social media, etc)? Do we really not have time, or is it that we just don't treasure God's wisdom more than the freedom to do what we want when we want?

Where can you create room to spend time with God daily?

I know I am hitting where it hurts, but if you really want to be wise, you have to seek God's wisdom like it is your greatest treasure. Proverbs 11:28 says, "Anyone trusting in his riches will fall, but the righteous will flourish like foliage."

What is your greatest treasure? What do you spend most of your time doing?

Have you ever seen those giant red numbers glowing on a lottery billboard and been tempted to pull off and pick up your own ticket? You know get rich scams are just that- scams. You know the chances of winning are extremely slim but the "what if" lingers in your mind. These kind of "what if's" get us in trouble. We dream about being the next Mark Zuckerberg, Steve Jobs, or Bill Gates. Or maybe you dream about becoming a YouTube sensation, Insta-Famous, or a big name travel blogger. Not many people get rich quick, but their lifestyles can be tempting.

I watched a show where one of the main characters won the lottery. At first, his life was a dream until he started to feel like people only loved him for his money. They always wanted something from him, and his life began to unravel. His fortune felt more like a curse than a blessing.

I've known real-life people with money who have shared these very same feelings. This is the side of wealth we don't imagine in our dreams. As I've watched friends become successful, I've noticed that becoming rich brings momentary elation, but maintaining the status quo seems just plain exhausting! An increase in wealth often means an increase of lifestyle. An increase of lifestyle means greater expenses, work, and worry.

I'm not against being successful or having money, but I am against money having you. Scripture says those who trust in the Lord are blessed (Jer. 17:5-8), and that wisdom brings life and joy (Prov. 3:13-18). When you ground your identity in Jesus rather than fame or fortune you will discover true joy.

How have you seen these truths in your own life?

What steps can you take to daily remind yourself of your identity in Jesus?

DAY 28
RICH IN GOOD DEEDS

When someone verbally instructs me, I zone out if their instructions become too complicated. I'm an experiential learner. If someone teaches me through a hands-on experience—seeing, feeling, hearing, or touching—I'll remember it forever. Spiritual lessons are no different. Have you ever listened to a sermon or bible teaching and thought, "I've got this concept nailed down." Then, when the situation visited you in real life, you failed miserably? I cannot tell you how many countless hours I've imagined soaring through a spiritual trial, but when the reality hit me, I messed up. Then I'd torture myself with all the ways I could or should have handled it until I wanted to give up.

Describe a similar experience in your own life.

Let me tell you how Jesus changed my defeatist mentality. He challenged me with this choice: You can wallow in your failures or learn from them and try again. You and I are on a spiritual journey. Each day Jesus gives us opportunities to live out what we are learning through life situations. Jesus isn't keeping a record of how many church services you've attended or how many verses you've memorized. Knowing the word is great, but knowing Jesus and applying His Word to your life is better (1 Cor. 8:1-2).

God doesn't expect you to make yourself perfect because that's His job. Your job is to listen to His instruction and put it into practice. Our spiritual development is an experiential learning journey. We learn as we do. We will not become who he has called us to be if we don't apply the lessons we learn. We can't apply the lessons we learn if we're too afraid to act on them. But the Holy Spirit will give you the strength to become rich in good deeds. The Lord goes before you, is with you, and will not leave you (Josh. 1:9).

How does this encourage you to walk in God's ways even after messing up?

Have you ever asked yourself why you are here? Why didn't God zip you up to heaven the minute you trusted Christ as your Savior?

> *Therefore, we are ambassadors for Christ, since God is making his appeal through us. We plead on Christ's behalf: "Be reconciled to God." 21 He made the one who did not know sin to be sin for us, so that in him we might become the righteousness of God.*
> —1 Corinthians 5:20-21

When we were saved, we immediately received two gifts: eternal life and the presence of the Holy Spirit. But we also get to be ambassadors for Christ to our world. The minute you understood and received salvation, God adopted you into His kingdom and you became a son or daughter of God. But there are people all around you who have not yet been reconciled to God. They were created to know God, but have not yet responded. As someone who has responded, you are a witness for God to the world around you.

> *Idle hands make one poor, but diligent hands bring riches. The son who gathers during summer is prudent; the son who sleeps during harvest is disgraceful.* —Proverbs 10:4-5

When I think of myself as an ambassador for Christ, I sometimes feel ashamed and convicted when I forget His commands or put them off. He asked me to spread His message, and I do, but I wonder if it's as high on my list of priorities as it is on His.

Read and meditate on 1 Corinthians 10:31 for a minute. Then ask yourself: Am I living out my calling as an ambassador to the glory of God? Am I giving this task my all?

If we want to be truly rich in faith, we have to accept all the responsibilities that come along with being a Christian, including our role as ambassadors for Christ.

RICH IN FAITH (PART 2)

When some people think about God, Jesus, Christianity, or religion, they remember all the do's and don'ts. When we consider the road we've walked with the Lord, we must admit obedience hasn't been easy. Still, He has given us innumerable rewards for following the road of wisdom.

I (Sharie) recently read the worldly stats for someone who has experienced a childhood like mine. There were multiple divorces and remarriages among my parents and step-parents, along with physical abuse and feelings of abandonment. However, the Holy Spirit has given me the wisdom to overcome the effects these situations could have inflicted on my soul.

With all the pain from my past, I could have become distracted by many false treasures. I could have chased men to fill my insecurity, success to prove my strength, or money to make me self-dependent. But, I chose to trust Jesus with my future, and as a result He has changed my future.

Statistics say someone like me should have dropped out of college, been married multiple times, and abused my children. But I graduated high school with a 4.15 GPA, have been married since 1999, and have two amazingly godly teenage sons whom I have never harmed. Nothing I could have chased could have given me this rich of a future, but I was only able to obtain them through the fear of the Lord and obedience to wisdom. A relationship with Jesus is not about a list of do's and don'ts. Following Jesus is a life of abundance that flows from a heart dedicated to making Him first.

When you ground yourself properly, God will bless you with more treasure than you could ask for or imagine (Eph. 3:20). If you're willing to give up the treasure of the world for the treasures of God's kingdom, you will have a future, and your hope will never fade. As Proverbs 13:11 says, "wealth obtained by fraud will dwindle, but whoever earns it through labor will multiply it." Chase the right treasure and you will reap an unbelievable reward.

SOURCES

SESSION 7

1. Andy Newman, "Lottery Winner Is Giving Her Millions Away," *The New York Times*, accessed August 13, 2018, https://www.nytimes.com/1997/11/10/nyregion/lottery-winner-is-giving-her-millions-away.html

2. Keith Caulfield, "Michael Jackson's 'Thriller' Extends Reign as Highest Certified Album in U.S. History," *Billboard*, February 16, 2017, https://www.billboard.com/articles/news/7693419/michael-jackson-thriller-highest-certified-album.

3. "Michael Jackson Net Worth," *Celebrity Net Worth*, accessed August 13, 2018, http://www.celebritynetworth.com/richest-celebrities/singers/michael-jackson-net-worth/.

4. Bill Finch, "The True Story of Kudzu, the Vine That Never Truly Ate the South," *Smithsonian.com*, September 2015, https://www.smithsonianmag.com/science-nature/true-story-kudzu-vine-ate-south-180956325/.

5. "Robin Williams's Biography," *IMDb*, http://m.imdb.com/name/nm0000245/quotes.

DEVOTIONS

1. David Lohr, "10 Most Notorious Criminals in American History," *Huffington Post*, December 6, 2017, https://www.huffingtonpost.com/2015/08/26/americas-most-notorious-criminals_n_3761487.html.